THE AWAKENING

Also by Ira Hirschmann:

Reflections On Music (with Arthur Schnabel)
Life Line To A Promised Land
The Embers Still Burn
Caution To The Wind
Red Star Over Bethlehem
Questions And Answers About Arabs And Jews

THE

AWAKENING

THE STORY OF THE
JEWISH NATIONAL FUND

by
Ira Hirschmann

SHENGOLD PUBLISHERS, INC.
NEW YORK

The author wishes to thank the following for permission to quote excerpts from:

Caution to the Winds, by Ira Hirschmann, copyright © 1962, by the David McKay Company, Inc. Reprinted by permission of the David McKay Company, Inc.

ISBN 0-88400-073-7
Library of Congress Catalog Card Number: 80-54447
Copyright © 1981 by Ira Hirschmann

Shengold Publishers, Inc., New York

PRINTED IN THE UNITED STATES OF AMERICA
TYPOGRAPHY BY NOVA TYPESETTING, REDMOND, WASHINGTON

This book is dedicated to
the memory of
Joseph Weitz
who shared with me his
devotion to the soil
of Israel

*Published on the occasion
of the 80th anniversary of
the founding of the
Jewish National Fund.*

Acknowledgements

I am obliged to a number of persons
who provided assistance in the
development of this book:

Rabbi William Berkowitz
Dr. Samuel I. Cohen
Milton Jacoby
Susan Suffes
Arie Y. Tamari
Lillian Rouse

I am indebted to
David Konoson
for his untiring
research and assistance

CONTENTS

What was the secret that gave the early settlers the courage to revive the desert?

That the soil is never dead; it is only tired and asleep.

It was the *awakening* of the soil that became the historic mission of the Jewish National Fund.

INTRODUCTION
by Rabbi William Berkowitz
President
Jewish National Fund

As a young student, I began the study of philosophy. Eager to explore the mystery of Jewish existence across the centuries, I delved into the minds of great thinkers. Each offered a distinct perspective, none too satisfying. Once older, I discovered a teacher who pointed to the Jewish preoccupation with time, as opposed to space. It was this aspect, he declared, which distinguished the Jewish People from others.

As a young Jew, I began the study of my people. Eager to explore the mystery of Jewish continuity in my own lifetime, I delved into the hearts of great Jews. I did not have to look too far. My own father, combined within his person the singular passions of a Jew of his era. Day in and day out, I heard him speak of space, of the Jewish obsession with a certain space. It was this aspect, he declared, which distinguished the Jewish People from others.

The two aspects, stark in their dialectical contradiction, stayed with me for many years to come. Did they ever achieve resolution? Perhaps only some months after June of 1967.

I remember the day: it was bright and sunny and I was tired from the long air journey. I walked down a plank of stairs and stood for the first time, on the dust of a faraway country, thousands of miles from New York, a country located on a small strip of land right off the Mediterranean. My mood, strange and awesome, made me think of many things but most especially: my father and my teacher. The one spoke of time, the other spoke of space. But somehow, at this moment, both made sense. For I had arrived in Israel, the only place in the world where time and space meet and embrace.

That summer I realized that when a Jew walks this land, brimming with sacred history, he encounters surprise. Each acre erupts in historic associations, each dunam reverberates with religious significance. For that matter, no one who stands on this soil can leave unmoved or untouched. Where else can one discover a living commentary on the Bible? Where else does archaeology yield theology and ancient tales offer contemporary instruction? And where else can one find a land whose very presence is a witness to hope, a cry against despair?

Because of this land, for 2,000 years an exiled people withstood resignation, and defying logic, believed that one day there would be a return. Look and you will see that no such attachment of a people to a land exists anywhere else in the world. The relationship is unprecedented and without analogy. How can one understand or explain it? Perhaps the answer lies in the Bible, the first written record of the union of Israel, the land and the people.

"Unto your seed will I give this Land.... And I will establish my covenant between me and you and between your seed after you in their generations... And I will give unto you and your seed after you the Land where you sojourn, all the Land of Canaan for an everlasting posssession and I will be their God..." says the Lord to Abraham, the first Jew.

The words, simple and clear, reveal that before there was a People, there was a Promise. The promise of a land. Nowhere in the entire traditions of humankind will you find another example of a 'promised land.' And it is doubtful whether you will find in another book of religious revelation, except the Bible, so much talk about a land. From the promises made to the Patriarchs to the warnings issued by the Prophets, wherever you look in the Bible, there you will find the land, Eretz Israel.

Eretz Israel: the place where the early figures found God, where they lived, where they died, where they were buried. Eretz Israel: the place where the People struggled to establish a kingdom, built two Temples, and where priests and prophets taught. Eretz Israel: the place where the promise of a land and the call to be a holy community were made one. It is a land that became the indispensable setting in which there was to be achieved a faith aimed at creating justice and holiness, closeness to God and closeness to man. For beyond the promise of the land, there was the fulfillment bound up with it. Ordained for the Jew, was a life that could not be realized by individuals in the sphere of private existence but only by a nation in the establishment of a certain society.

For the Jew then, from the very beginning, Zion was
not a symbol but a home. Before it became an image, it
was a real place. And that maybe explains why the Jew
never stopped talking of Eretz Israel, even after the
days of the Bible. So important was it to the Rabbis, that
one-third of the Mishnah, the primary Jewish legal text
is devoted to the land alone. And so dear was it to the
Rabbis, that they simply referred to it as, Ha-Aretz, The
Land. Whether in law or legend, in their universe, there
was only one land, The Land, Ha-Aretz, and everything
else was Chutz La-Aretz, Outside The Land. To dwell in
The Land, they said, ranked equally in merit with all
other commandments. And for them, that commandment was eternal, abiding in each and every generation.

And yet, circumstance interfered with commandment.
In the year 70 of this era, Jerusalem was destroyed and
the Jewish People were driven into exile. From then on,
the Jews could no longer dwell in The Land: The Land
had to dwell in them. And this it did, through deed, devotion, dedication. Scattered throughout the world, this
people never lost sight of its ancestral home. No matter
how far or how dispersed, every individual was united by
a single geographic center, connected by the same
dream of restoration. Everything was just like before,
only now with one crucial difference. Henceforth, he
who could not rebuild or return in space, rebuilt and
returned in time. The promise which had become place,
now became prayer and passion.

And so for the next nineteen centuries, it was Jewish
law and custom that articulated the fierce union
between the Jewish People and the Land of Israel. From
womb to tomb, the Jew was surrounded by his love for

The Land. When a newborn child was welcomed into the community, he was blessed with the hope that he might become worthy to be a pilgrim to The Land. When the same child married, the blessings which marked the event referred to Zion, even as ashes were placed on his forehead and a glass smashed, two acts meant to recall the destruction and exile. And when the same person died, a small sack of earth from The Land was put in the grave under his head, while the mourners were consoled with a phrase that joined their sorrow to that of Zion and Jerusalem.

Beyond the life cycle, the image of Zion permeated the everyday life of the People. Three times daily in prayer, Jerusalem was recalled and evoked whether in word or gesture. When one commenced the worship, which contained numerous references to a rebuilt Zion, one turned East toward The Land. Think of it: for thousands of years, wherever Jews resided, whether Yemen or Egypt, Poland or Russia, Brazil or South Africa, Germany or England, Morocco or America, thrice daily they turned their bodies in the direction of Zion. "Every step I take, I take toward Jerusalem" said Rabbi Nachman of Bratzlav, expressing a central conviction of millions of Jews.

Even mealtimes was an occasion for recall. In the blessings of gratitude, recited after every meal, Jerusalem and Zion were remembered and prayers were offered for their restoration (do you know any other people that remembers a faraway country after they have eaten?) One commentator, obviously himself lovesick for The Land, explained the custom which requires the removal of knives from the table at grace-time as being a measure to prevent despairing Jews from plunging the knives into their hearts at even the mention of a forlorn Jerusalem!

The Jewish calendar also served as a cord binding the Jew to his land. As each new month was inaugurated, special prayers for The Land were offered. At various times throughout the year, prayers for rain and dew were recited but with one twist: the prayers were in accord with the seasons of The Land rather than referring to the climates of the lands in which the worshippers recited the prayers! Indeed, every holiday, holy-day, and fast-day had some referent to Zion. For that matter, the very calendar itself and calculation of holidays, was fixed according to The Land. Seasons, too uttered Zion's name. In Fall, great care and funds were expended in order to purchase special citrons from The Land. In Winter, a fast day and a feast day were devoted to The Land. The latter, called Tu B'Shvat was a time for planting trees in The Land and the eating of special fruits and produce in an unique ceremony. In Spring, at the Passover seder, the conclusion was a triumphant shout of 'Next year in Jerusalem' followed by 49 days recalling the ancient harvest of The Land. And in Summer, there began a major three week period of mourning for the exile and destruction, culminating in the 24 hour fasting period of Tisha B'Av.

In homes, Zion was vividly recalled, too. For centuries Jews left part of their abodes undone and unbuilt, in order to remind themselves of exile and that wherever they lived outside The Land, they were less than whole.

A devotional object called the *Mizrach,* which literally means The East, adorned the walls of many homes in order to orient one's daily consciousness towards The Land. The Shabbat, the Sabbath, was usually the occasion when travelers who came from The Land were most eagerly sought, welcomed and accorded great hospitality. Even before the Sabbath began and the candles were lit, charity was given for the upbuilding of The Land and the support of its brave inhabitants in whatever the era. And for centuries, even until present times, many Jews would rise at midnight each night (but the Sabbath) to mourn and lament over the destruction and exile.

Outside the home, in the study halls, students would eagerly learn those portions of traditional literature which dealt with the Temple and the laws concerning The Land while among the religious judges and decisors numerous cases would rise involving The Land. One example: an early source in Jewish legal literature states that one may sign a bill of sale on the Sabbath in order to conclude the purchase of a home in The Land. So great was this opportunity, that an action which was strictly prohibited on the Sabbath was set aside and permitted!

One could write entire volumes documenting the intense relationship of the Jew and Zion and how it was lived out on a daily level. The examples of it are endless, for the love was unceasing, the yearning uncontrollable. Indeed, for years and years, century after century, this was the picture which portrayed the Jew and Zion.

And then one day, in the nineteenth century, something uncontrollable, something we don't really understand, took hold of all the prayers and all the pleas and all the words and all the gestures, and a People, trembling under the realization of a dream about to come to life, began the long awaited return home. It would take nearly a century before the world took notice of The Return and officially recognized it. And while The Return would have to become a diplomatic mission and even a military conflict, at its core it was a spiritual adventure. The movement home, preceding Theodor Herzl himself, began with young people whose souls were inextricably bound with the soil. Each pioneer became a pilgrim, each one a trailblazer amidst terrifying frontiers. The names were different but the story was the same: hundreds and hundreds of Eastern European young men and women, threw caution to the winds and abandoning family and comfort alike, sought salvation amidst the malaria-ridden marshlands of the Middle East. Skeptics and sympathizers alike scoffed at their efforts, but their determination triumphed and taught the world that the impossible is possible and that which is unbelievable can come true. Their saga, in all its detail, remains largely unknown, except to the most devoted of their disciples. Ira Hirschmann has told that remarkable tale with depth and passion in this small yet important volume. All who will read it will go away amazed at these pioneers and their tenacity, of their rebellion against geography, of their power of will over logic. For theirs is a wondrous tale, spanning the River Babylon and River Basle, a tale of struggle and triumph, of joy and caution, of lullabies sung to small children and assurances given to old men.

And yes, it is a tale of time and space, a tale of teachers and fathers both, a tale of my teacher and my

father both, a tale which links me, student and son, to
their memory, and beyond.

AUTHOR'S FOREWORD

On returning from Turkey to the U.S. in 1945, at the conclusion of my mission for President Roosevelt, I stopped off in Jerusalem to see some of the Jewish children I had helped rescue from Nazi-held territory, via the Bosphorus and Istanbul. I also wanted to exchange diplomatic notes with David Ben-Gurion and visit with Henrietta Szold, the mother of Hadassah, who had welcomed the children to their new home.

While in Jerusalem, I made a striking discovery. I learned the true meaning of the little blue box that had served as a receptacle for extra coins on the mantle in my childhood home in Baltimore. How could I have known as a boy that these small token steps would stretch into strides for land purchases that would provide the foundation and backbone of the new state of Israel?

It was the impact on that visit of the incredible creative work of the Jewish National Fund in transforming sand and rock into cultivated soil that sparked my determination. It served as a summons for me to join the dedicated men and women who guided the program of the JNF* in

---

* In Israel (Hebrew) Keren Kayemeth LeIsrael

the United States. I have been a member of the Board of the JNF ever since.

One of my most vivid memories came back to me:

"Near the Egyptian border at the Gaza Strip, I watched an Israeli girl planting flowers. On her knees in front of her small, prefabricated two-room house, she patiently sifted the soil through her fingers, separating the stones from the sand. Then, holding her flowers tenderly, she set their roots in shallow holes she had scooped out of the newly restored earth. Doling out drops of precious water, she tamped down the ground with her hands, patting the soil almost as lovingly as one would handle a newborn child. As I watched this girl perform her act of love for the soil, I thought that here was the symbol of Israel — a portent of clover in the desert."*

No instinct of man, no goal, is more pervasive and unrelenting than the drive to engage in the search for undiscovered regions. The man who will hesitate to set a foot across a crowded traffic street, will plot with maps and assorted equipment to climb Mount Everest. The "never-never" land is a never-ending challenge.

Less dramatic but no less eventful has been the relentless struggle against the vast barren deserts (62% of the earth's surface) of the pioneer Jew. Persecuted, scattered over many lands for over 2,000 years, these people saw the seemingly endless desert as a temporary barrier to be overcome and prepared for the return to a

---

* From *Caution to the Winds* by the author

"homeland." The Romans, the Turks for 400 years, and the British all turned away in the face of vast, endless scenes of sand and rock which only taunted them in their futile efforts to give the wasteland some meaning or value.

How was it that a relative handful of people, disenfranchised, uprooted from their homes, managed to sustain an unbroken will to transform a barren wasteland into life-giving soil to yield its hidden treasures of vegetation, food and even water below the sands — not thorns but flowers?

Perhaps for the Jew to recover the land was to rediscover himself; to hear the secret from an inner spirit kept alive by a faith that the message from the Mount was no shibboleth, no empty promise, no elusive dream — but the reality that sprang from the original "Word":

"And I will give unto thee, and to thy seed after thee, the land wherein thou art a stranger, all the land of Canaan, for an everlasting possession."*

"..a land flowing with milk and honey."**

Were the Jews not the custodians of the Law? Then why not the Land? The soil, barren or fertile, is nevertheless God's creation. Being men of God they could keep it alive. To make it fertile was to embrace it, to give its life back to it. If little light was offered to the Jew from

---

* Genesis 17:8
** Exodus 3:8

his shadowed ghetto in Eastern Europe, from his minority status in the Arab villages, the illumination from the "Book" would never lose its glow.

With the creation of the Jewish National Fund, the Jews re-entered history in a new role. The repossession of the land would prepare them for their homeland and the founding of a new State. In this book, the JNF blueprint for the new State, its contribution to technology and farming the world over, its destiny as a continuing, indispensible vehicle for the nation's healthy growth is brought to light as part of her modern identity.

Thus it has become the role of the JNF to express the timelessness that enshrines the history of a free people reunited in the land of their forefathers.

Theodor Herzl *(1860–1904) founder of modern political Zionism, addressing the Fifth Zionist Congress in Basle, Switzerland, on December 29, 1901. It was at this meeting that the historic JNF program was adopted when he proclaimed "the establishment of a National Fund . . . the Jewish people shall not only set up this Fund, but shall also control its disposition in perpetuity."*

I
THE DREAM

The setting: Basle, Switzerland. The scene: Stadkasino Hall. The time: December 26, 1901. The gathering: 197 Jewish leaders from America, England, France, Germany, Austro-Hungary, Bulgaria, Serbia, Roumania, Palestine and Scandavia. They had come a long way, far in miles but even farther as measured by vision and faith.

The great hall is full to suffocation. Long before the opening all seats are occupied. Here and there groups are forming; one hears every possible European language spoken. The festively decorated hall shows the blue and white* banner. The Star of David destined to become the flag of Israel has been unfurled.

What could have been the thoughts and visions of those 197 dedicated men awaiting the sound of the gavel in the hand of Theodor Herzl as he stood on a platform

---

* The colors were those of the Biblical fringes: Num. 15,18.

literally poised on the edge of history? Could these eager delegates have sensed that a memorable moment for world Jewry was to be written, that the instrument to be created on this day would be the means of acquiring the land that would become the foundation of the new-born state of the Jews?

The gavel sounded. Herzl, bearded, eyes aflame, stood erect, his voice commanding and incisive:

> "...And now...we can proceed to the execution of the plan submitted to the Congress by our deceased friend, Hermann Schapira, Professor at the Heidelberg University: the establishment of a National Fund...the Jewish people shall not only set up this Fund, but shall also control its disposition in perpetuity."*

The author of the plan, Hermann Schapira** at the First Zionist Congress in 1897, had stamped it with a vision that gave it a quality of timelessness.

> "A Fund must be set up by the Jewish people of the world to redeem the soil of Eretz Israel.

---

* Herzl's diary of November 8, 1896 had anticipated his historic words: "I am suggesting the establishment of a Jewish National Fund which is to make us independent of the bankers...in all places where Jews reside, the JNF should be started through collections, donations, etc."

** Professor Schapira was born in Lithuania in 1840 and ordained a Rabbi at the age of 24. In later years he studied in London, Berlin, and Heidelberg where he became a professor of mathematics. He was an active member of the "Lovers of Zion," a movement of the 19th century which sought both return to the land and work on its soil.

It is imperative that every Jew, young old, rich
or poor, without distinction, should be able to
participate in this general Jewish fund. The
land thus purchased shall be forever the property of the National Fund...and shall not be
sold to individuals, but shall be leased to those
who work it for a period of not more than 49
years..."

Among the delegates who addressed the Congress
was Israel Zangwill, the noted author:

"We are being told: Zionism is a dream. How
could it be otherwise, since the Jews are
asleep? Should the Jews awake, then it will be
a dream no longer...As I said about Palestine,
'Give the land without a people to the people
without a land.' "

"Use your money only in order to make
ready a home for our wandering people. Our
last home lies, alas, in ruins and wreckage and,
still, if it had not been in decay, it would not
have been empty of people and waiting for us.
No alms to the Jews, but their participation in
the agricultural and industrial development of
Palestine."

The next morning, Delegate Uriassohn stated to the
Congress:

"Schapira said that if the idea of the National
Fund became a reality, he could die in peace. I
say on the contrary: If the National Fund exists, then I can live in peace."

Delegate Dr. Awompwotzlo added:

> "We should take an example from nature.
> What does nature create? It first makes a cell,
> an embryo, and out of these comes a being. We
> should create the cells."

Numerous delegates then approached the Chairman's podium, in order to hand in monetary contributions for the Jewish National Fund.

Dr. Bodenheimer, another delegate, explained his contribution, in the name of the students of Heidelberg University:

> "Thanks to the untiring activity of our highly
> respected comrade, Dr. Schapira, a society
> had been formed in Heidelberg already some
> years ago which is statutorily obliged to collect
> money for the National Fund. The amounts
> have been collected by students, penny by pen-
> ny, and they are available in Heidelberg. I am
> authorized to remit this amount, a little over
> 2,000 marks, to the National Fund on behalf of
> the German organizations."

The Chairman then quoted "a long time proposal by Professor Schapira":

> "Let us imagine that our ancestors had
> secured at the time of their departure into ex-
> ile an amount, be it ever so little, for future
> times. We could then have acquired with it to-
> day greater territories. What our ancestors in

part could not, or in part neglected to do, we are obliged to do, for ourselves and for our descendants...Contributions towards the establishment of a general Jewish fund should be collected from Jews all over the world, without any distinction, whether they be poor or rich...The territory acquired should never be alienated and not even sold to individual Jews, but can only be leased and then, at most, for 49 years..."

The most significant provision in the declaration of the JNF in 1901 was that the land purchased should *forever* remain the property of *all* the Jewish people everywhere. Under no circumstances was it to be sold again. This provided a timeless and universal quality to the ownership of the land. This was based on the Bible: "The Land shall not be sold forever for the Land is Mine." (Leviticus 25,23)

Jewish National Fund lands were to be leased for periods of 49 years, and the contracts were subject to renewal for another 49 years, based on the Biblical tradition of the Jubilee or 50th year, during which all land is to be returned to its original owners.*

What had occurred on that day at the turn of the century was a central irreversible step in Jewish history. A few men, motivated by ancient prophesy and future

---

* "And ye shall hallow the 50th year, and proclaim liberty throughout the land unto all the inhabitants thereof; it shall be a jubilee unto you; and ye shall return every man unto his family." (Leviticus 25, 10)

need, drew together to forge an instrument that would permit a people to stand once again on their own soil.

The plan for a people's Fund for Land would prove to be the means by which pioneer settlers would take the first firm steps, not only to reclaim the desert but to embrace it and make it fruitful once again as part of an imperishable heritage. The high price to be paid would be a pittance against the reward awaiting them, a dream so close to fulfillment on this day that they could behold it but hardly grasp it.

Herzl's Statesmanship

The historic meeting in Basle in 1901 was the climax of the years of ferment that had preceded it arising out of the concept of purchase of the land and settlements. As far back as 1839, Sir Moses Montefiore*, a British, Jewish philanthropist, contemplated leasing land in Palestine from Mohammed Ali, ruler of Turkey, to form a company for cultivation of the land and to encourage Jews to return to Palestine.

On a visit to Palestine in 1855, Sir Moses bought land near Jaffa that was turned into the first Jewish orange plantation. He also purchased land outside the walls of the Old City of Jerusalem where he built a housing pro-

---

* (1784–1885) Philanthropist, Jewish communal leader and supporter of Palestine projects. A member of a well-to-do family in Italy, he was brought to England in infancy and became one of London's most successful financiers. In 1826 he retired from business to devote all his time to Jewish communal and philanthropic work. Throughout his life he not only gave large amounts of money to charity but also interceded with rulers and governments for the rights of Jews the world over, and actively worked for the welfare of the Jews of Palestine.

ject for the poor which became the first Jewish residential section in that part of Jerusalem.

In the last years of Montefiore's life the Hovevei Zion (Lovers of Zion) movement came into being. The movement's origin in 1882 was a direct reaction to the widespread pogroms in Russia of 1881, for the purpose of encouraging Jewish settlement in Palestine towards a Jewish National revival there. Its founders had been influenced by writers such as Rabbi Zvi Hirsch Kalischer* and A. David Gordon.** They were also influenced by the Balkan nations' struggle for independence. In 1879 Eliezer Ben Yehuda (pioneer of the restoration of Hebrew as a living language) wrote: "If the Jews are to survive as a people, a Jewish National Home will have to be created in Palestine."

The growth of the movement was quickened also by the unfavorable conditions under which the Jews of Eastern Europe lived. Pogroms and the denial of civil rights in Russia, persecution and economic pressures in Romania, led to Jewish emigration from those countries and strengthened the concept of settlement in the Land of Israel. Smaller Hovevei Zion groups were established in Austria-Hungary, England, and the United States.

As the pioneer Jewish Palestine settlement organization, the Hovevei Zion was the forerunner of modern Zionism. Professor Hermann Schapira was an active

---

* (1795–1874) a noted Prussian rabbi who wrote in 1862 the first Hebrew book to appear in Eastern Europe on the subject of modern Jewish agricultural settlement in Palestine.

** (1831–1886) a Hebrew publicist in Russia who tirelessly advocated the establishment of Jewish agricultural settlements in Palestine.

member of the Hovevei Zion from which he derived his concept of a Jewish National Fund.

It was the expose of anti-Semitism in the famous Dreyfus case in Paris in 1894 which awakened the Jewish consciousness of one man who was inspired to found the movement that became modern, political Zionism. Theodor Herzl, a journalist and playwright, was born in Budapest in 1860 into a well-to-do merchant's family with only a superficial background in Jewish culture and its affairs. He studied law at the University of Vienna, but soon turned to a literary career, attaining a reputation for his charming novelettes and diverting plays which won him the important position in 1891 of Paris Correspondent of the Vienna newspaper, the "Neue Freie Presse," then the most influential publication in Central Europe.

When, three years later, at the trial of Captain Alfred Dreyfus on a trumped-up charge of treason, Herzl reported the proceedings for his paper, he was witness to the dramatic episodes that led to the degradation and banishment of the martyred Jew, along with its accompanying outbursts of anti-Semitic hostility.

Herzl saw the revival of anti-Semitism as a personal affront, forcing him for the first time to become conscious of his Jewish heritage. He came to the conclusion that the sole solution of the problem for Jews and non-Jews alike was the establishment of an internationally recognized Jewish state. This inspired him to write *Der Judenstaat* (The Jewish State) which appeared in 1896. The book took the Jewish world by storm. The Hovevei Zion (Lovers of Zion) were at first divided in their attitude towards the book, fearing that it would alarm the Turkish Government which might discontinue further

Jewish colonizing in Palestine. But the majority soon rallied to Herzl's side, followed by many others.

Herzl travelled far and wide in an attempt to meet and obtain support from political leaders for his scheme. He visited the Grand Duke of Baden in an unsuccessful effort at approaching the German Emperor. He then met with the Grand Vizier in Constantinople, but was unable to meet with the Sultan. A visit to Baron Edmond de Rothschild proved equally fruitless. Despite his generous interest in the Jewish resettlement of Palestine, Rothschild was apprehensive of any politically oriented program.

Herzl came to the realization that in only one way could he hope to secure practical cooperation: through the democratic method of calling a congress of representatives of the Jewish people. A monumental idea, it was the first such gathering in eighteen hundred years — since the exile of Jews from Palestine. Munich was at first selected as a convenient meeting place, but the heads of the local Jewish community protested against what they regarded as a slur upon their national loyalty. The city of Basle in Switzerland was then chosen.

In spite of serious obstacles, Herzl succeeded in convening the First Zionist Congress on August 27, 1897. It lasted three days. It was at this meeting that the historic Zionist program was adopted that proclaimed "The aim of Zionism is to create for the Jewish people a home in Palestine secured by public law." It was there that Professor Herman Schapira first projected his proposal — to create a National Fund for the purchase of land in Palestine, which was adopted in the Fifth Zionist Congress in 1901.

Hermann Schapira *(1840–1898) creator of the concept of the Jewish National Fund. At the First Zionist Congress (1897) he first projected his proposal—to create a National Fund for the purchase of land in Palestine. His suggestion that the fund should be based on the Biblical principle of leasing and not selling the land to individuals was adopted when the Jewish National Fund was established in 1901.*

II
THE AWAKENING: THE PLOW AND THE RIFLE

Return to the soil figured prominently in the thought of Zionist dreamers in the middle of the 19th century. The yearning of the Jew for his land had never deserted him. For him it became an article of faith. In Rabbi Yehuda Alkalay of Bodnia's words: "When the people of Israel begin to work the land, that means the end of dispersion."

Farming had been the principal occupation of the Jew until the 7th century when he was evicted from his land. But in the Jewish tradition, farming never died. A large part of Talmudic law is devoted to agriculture and nearly every sentence is related to farming. Throughout the generations that followed, the intimate association with the soil was repeated by the Jews in their prayers. The religious festivals were connected with agriculture: on Shavuot, when the farmers were ready to gather the wheat harvest, they could offer sacrifices and prayers to the God of heaven and earth who made the harvest possible; on Succoth, at one time called "the Feast of the Ingathering," the fruit harvest was blessed; on Passover, prayers for the fall of dew at night to substitute for rain in the dry season echoed in synagogues all over the world.

In the 1880's a few hundred Jews, members of the "Lovers of Zion," established three pioneer colonies: Rishon Le Zion, Zikhron Yaakov, and Rosh Pina. When faced by the problem of insufficient funds, it was Baron Edmond de Rothschild of Paris who came to their rescue and financed the colonies. Banker, patron of scientific and cultural projects, developer and supporter of Palestine projects, Baron Rothschild (1845-1934) was, from his earliest youth, concerned with Jewish problems. In 1882, following the pogroms in Russia, he first became interested in the Palestine settlement work of the Hovevei Zion movement. To save the new settlement Rishon Le Zion from financial collapse, Rothschild donated 30,000 francs, and subsequently took under his wing Rosh Pina and Zikhron Ya'akov. Altogether, he invested 5,600,000 English pounds (27 million dollars; 8 million dollars between 1885 and 1889).

Wine grapes were the chief product of the first colonists, which Baron Rothschild had started by building the wine cellars of Rishon Le Zion and Zikhron Ya'akov. Rothschild was guided by the idea that agriculture in

Palestine should follow the pattern of that in southern France since the soil and climate were similar. This meant giving perference to vineyards over the cultivation of grain. The vines from abroad, however, were found to be unsuitable for local cultivation. Since there was no market for the wine, Rothschild suffered heavy losses and the colonies ultimately shifted to the cultivation of grain.

To compensate for the Jewish settlers' lack of experience, Baron Rothschild sent French administrators to manage the farms. These "overseers," completely alien to the spirit of the "Lovers of Zion," despised the settlers both for their stubborn attachment to the land and for their clumsiness at work. The administrators began interfering in the settlers' personal lives, treating them as charity seekers. The spirit of the settlers suffered. Forced to hire cheap Arab labor, little by little the new Jewish peasants assumed the habits of small-scale landlords. Only later did the Jews become farm laborers. After the Second Immigration of 1904, workers used to physical work from East-European backgrounds, came to help the settlers.

Though they had come to the country with the express intention of standing on their own feet without having to rely on philanthropy, the settlers found themselves completely dependent on Baron Rothschild. Unable to exercise autonomy, some of them formed a small group called *Menucha V' Nachala* ("Rest and Heritage"). Its purpose was to establish a cooperative colony which would be entirely independent of Rothschild's aid and tutelage. The colony of Rehovot was subsequently founded by this group and was the only settlement established between 1882 and 1892 that operated without the Baron's administrators. It was based on a system of cooperation and mutual aid among its members.

In 1904, the JNF acquired its first land holdings in the country: Ben Shemen (375 acres) and Hulda (500 acres), both in the Judean foothills. The immediate problem was how to put this land to use. Professor Otto Warburg, one of the leading Zionists of the time, proposed planting olive trees which, in his words, "give fruit and stand out by their longevity." A special olive tree fund was set up by the JNF and contributions were received from many parts of the world. After Herzl's death in the summer of 1904, it was decided that those trees should be planted in his memory. Thus the Herzl Forest was born.

In 1905, the JNF purchased 500 acres in the Lower Galilee, and in 1908 a tract of 1,625 acres was bought in the Jordan Valley. These later became the site of the settlements of Degania and Kinneret. Kinneret was then set up as a training farm by Dr. Arthur Ruppin,* Director of Zionist settlement work, to prepare Jewish laborers for settlements of their own.

---

* Zionist leader and organizer of agricultural settlement in Palestine (1876–1943). An eminent sociologist, Dr. Ruppin served in the period 1908–1914, as head of the Palestine Office of the Zionist Organization in Jaffa. In this capacity he directed all practical JNF work in the country, setting up the Palestine Land Development Company (PLDC) through which important tracts of land were acquired for the JNF. In 1920 he advocated, and carried through, together with M.M. Ussishkin and Yehoshua Hankin, the decisively important purchase of the Jezreel Valley lands (between Haifa and the Jordan Valley). He also devised for the country the concept of mixed farming (planting more than one crop) and was an ardent supporter of the new forms of communal and cooperative settlement.

The first settlers to cultivate JNF land were housed in a one-room Arab inn, which served both as sleeping and living quarters as well as the storage room for their equipment. Only after several months, was the one room increased to six. A number of the workers were soon incapacitated by disease, especially malaria. Neighboring *fellahin* (Arab peasants) and Bedouins made frequent attacks on the group. The plow and the rifle were both used to conquer the soil and protect it.

Shmuel Dayan, father of Moshe Dayan, former Defense Minister and Foreign Minister of Israel, described the hardships of the early farm laborers:

"Despite the certainty and faith that filled our hearts, we were sometimes assailed with doubts. We had a difficult task to perform. Malaria still sapped our strength and weakened our bodies; the work itself was by no means easy. Our bodies wearied, our feet stumbled, our heads ached. Our food was meagre and of poor quality, and the sun was pitilessly hot and weakened us still more...Sometimes we faltered, but we stayed on, telling ourselves that this was all we had to cling to. We strove to the limit of our strength and this striving gave us courage — and we won."*

The first work of the settlement was the improvement of the land without the assistance of any machinery. It was a crucible test of the pioneers. It involved weeding, removal of stones and boulders, and deep plowing, sometimes with bare hands. The main crop sown was wheat, but part of the land was planted with green fodder, potatoes, and other vegetables.

---

*Shmuel Dayan, *Pioneers in Israel*, The World Publishing Co., Cleveland, Ohio, 1961.

By February of 1909 there were 43 men and women employed at the Kinneret settlement. It was because the workers insisted they did not have sufficient influence on the decisions of the manager that Dr. Ruppin permitted them to form a JNF settlement on the east bank of Lake Kinneret. Their success exceeded all expectations which brought a new group of workers to settle there in 1910, changing the name to Degania, the first kvutzah (small kibbutz) or collective settlement in the country.

It was the readiness of the JNF to experiment with new social patterns that resulted in the creation of a type of settlement uniquely suited to Israel's special conditions and not duplicated elsewhere in the world: the kibbutz. A collective governed by all of its members, the kibbutz is based on the unimpeachable principle, "From each according to his ability, to each according to his need." Its property is controlled by all those who belong to the kibbutz and is not based on shareholding. Work that the members perform on a cooperative basis is returned to them in housing, food, clothing and social services, but not in ownership of the land. Different types of kibbutzim exist, each stemming from religious, political, and ideological origins.

Another form of settlement created at this time was the moshav, or cooperative farming village. Unlike the kibbutz, each member family of the moshav has its own farm, but a central cooperative is the medium through which all supplies are bought and all produce sold. A general assembly of the moshav elects a council which approves all transfers of farms and accepts new members. The concept of the moshav was first introduced in Merhavia (the first plot of land acquired in the Jezreel Valley), in 1911. Along with the kibbutz, the moshav set the pattern for practically all the subsequent agricultural settlements based on land provided by the Jewish National Fund.

It was the low wages of the Arabs in the villages with which Jewish laborers could not compete that led to the origin of the moshav. In order to help the Jewish workers to subsist, homes and farms were provided for them on JNF land (En Ganim near Petah Tikvah, Nahlat Yehuda near Rishon le Zion and others). When some of the laborers abandoned their jobs to work on their farms, they joined together and formed what became moshavim.

Since the land the JNF acquired was not fit for agriculture, it meant clearing away stones and rocks, draining swamps, and restoring the soil for cultivation. The back-breaking work of reclaiming the soil became one of the first and major projects of the JNF. The settlers were able to obtain land practically rent-free from the JNF, which at the time depended on the laborers to occupy the barren stretches of terrain it had acquired. Only the dedicated and energetic work of the settlers in reclaiming the soil enabled the JNF to maintain its right to the ownership of the land it had purchased. Had these remained wastelands for an extended period of time, the JNF's claim of proprietorship would have become invalid under Turkish laws which remained in effect until Great Britain was given a mandate over the region by the League of Nations in 1922.

The Ottoman Empire was the government that had ultimate control of the land with regulations that purchasers were obliged to obey for 400 years (1517-1918). Every landowner was required to have his property inscribed in an official record called the Turkish Land

Register. According to Ottoman law, any land suitable for cultivation which was left uncultivated for three successive years was confiscated by the State. This law became a dead letter after the 1922 mandate.

Besides the concern for the Turkish laws and the inhospitality of the land, the settlers had to contend with the hostility of the Arabs. The Arabs watched every step taken by the Jews, ready to exploit through theft, robbery, or direct attack any sign of weakness. Their intention was to frighten the Jewish settlers away and take possession of their property. The redemption of every dunam (¼ acre) of land was made possible, not only through JNF purchases but by the blood and suffering of the settlers.

It was the funds made available by the Jewish National Fund that enabled a suburb of Jaffa, a Mediterranean seaport, to be founded; and to become the city of Tel Aviv.

At the outset of Zionist immigration in the beginning of the century, the Jewish population of Jaffa under Turkish rule numbered about 5,000. It quickly increased. The Jews of Jaffa lived either in non-Jewish quarters or in old-fashioned, cramped, and unsanitary conditions which induced a group of sixty Jews, consisting of merchants, teachers, and others to strive for the establishment of a new and more habitable Jewish suburb outside Jaffa.

In 1907 they approached the JNF to lend them 12,000 pounds and asked Dr. Ruppin to support their request. He inspected the proposed site—a derelict, sandy waste north of Jaffa—and found it suitable. In a letter to the JNF, Ruppin stated that he attached the greatest importance to the idea of founding a new Jewish suburb. "The narrow streets, lack of sanitation, and strange style of building in the existing Jewish quarters," he wrote, "are a positive disgrace to the Jews, and deter many civilized people from settling in this country." He stressed his conviction of the soundness of the project and recommended the granting of the loan.

A few weeks later the JNF issued the loan in the amount of 10,000 pounds, and by June, 1909, the plans were prepared and building commenced. A year later most of the members of the group were installed in their new homes. The quarter, which consisted of small houses—mostly one per family—surrounded by gardens and intersected by a broad street, was called by Ruppin "one of the finest and most successful achievements created by Zionism in Palestine."

Tel Aviv is now the largest city in Israel, with a population of 348,500.

Arthur Ruppin *(1876–1943) An eminent sociologist, he was a Zionist leader and innovator of agricultural settlement in Palestine. As head of the Palestine Office of the Zionist Organization in Jaffa (1908–1914), he was an ardent supporter of the new forms of communal and cooperative settlement, directing practical JNF work in the country and acquiring important tracts of land.*

III

WHO OWNED THE LAND

"The Land of Milk and Honey" aptly described the vast areas as they flourished in biblical days. A measure of the unceasing despoilation, neglect, and desctruction of the land can be seen in the endless waste and desert that the pioneers faced in their return from exile. The primary cause for the barren and deteriorated condition of the land which prevailed from the seventh century to the 1922 British Mandate was the agrarian provision of the Islamic Code, followed by the Ottoman Code, which controlled the area. Under the Codes, the land was to be divided among all the children in succeeding generations. The land was thus continually fragmented into smaller and smaller parcels. These subdivisions did not provide a broad enough acreage for cultivation. The result was desolation, neglect, and devastation of the countryside. In addition to this, unending warfare over the centuries devastated the countryside. In the period following the Crusades, the Mameluke rulers systematically destroyed everything in the Coastal Plain to bar the way of fresh invasions from the sea. The spread of pestilential malaria, along with the unceasing molestation and pillaging of the peasants by the Bedouins, caused the virtual desertion of the northern Negev and nearly all of Transjordan.

The land purchased by the JNF required the gigantic task of reclamation from the ground up. From 1901 to 1948 the local landowners sold only the barren or rocky portions of their holdings to the JNF. From absentee landlords, large tracts were purchased which had been neglected or previouly uncultivated. The charge later made by Arabs that the Jews had obtained too large a portion of good land was refuted in the British Royal Commission Report of 1937: "Much of the land now carrying orange groves was sand dunes or swamps and uncultivated when it was purchased." Hundreds of millions of dollars were paid by the JNF for the purchase of land from 1880 to 1947, often at exhorbitant prices. In 1944 they paid $1,000 to $1,100 per acre for mostly arid or semi-arid land. (That same year, according to the United States Department of Agriculture, rich, black soil in Iowa was selling for $110 dollars per acre.)

Before 1918 at least 71% of the land now Israel had been public lands controlled for 400 years by the Ottoman Empire. By the end of the second decade of the twentieth century at least 75% of the available non-public land was in the hands of about 300 to 400 owners.

Of the hundreds of thousands of Arab fellaheen (peasants), only a very small number owned any land. The rest were tenant farmers on land owned by big landowners.

Prior to 1947, the Jews purchased 18,500,000 dunams (about 4,650,000 acres) in Palestine. Practically all of this was within the area that later became Israel. It was mostly bought by the Jewish National Fund. The Palestine Jewish Colonization Association and the Palestine Land Development Company also purchased land. The holdings of these three agencies were bought for the purpose of distribution among the kibbutzim and moshavim. A large tract was purchased by Baron Edmond de Rothschild.

More than half—52.6%—was bought from absentee landowners who did not even live in Palestine. Many were not Arabs. About a quarter —24.6%—was purchased from large landowners living in Palestine. Another 13.4% was purchased from the Turkish government, churches, foreign firms, and individual wealthy businessmen with small holdings. Less than a tenth—9.4%—was purchased from Arab fellaheen who as a group constituted 95% of the population.

The grip of power of the Ottoman Empire on the area now known as the Middle East was based on its control of the land. Due to corruption among Turkish officials, however, lands could be acquired either through personal connections, influence or with the help of *baksheesh* (bribes).

The Turks displayed intense animosity toward Jewish settlement in Palestine. They imposed a dual prohibition on Jews, forbade their entry for permanent residence in

the country, and would not allow their purchase of land.
Turkey feared nationalist ambitions such as had led to
the liberation of the Balkans and the uprising of the
Armenians. Government ordinances, issued in 1882 and
again in 1891, forbade Jews to enter Palestine except on
short visits. Usually, with the aid of a bribe, it was possible to purchase the "connivance" of the authorities and
remain on the land permanently. Almost every activity,
from purchasing land to the erection of buildings
depended upon the attitude of Turkish junior government officials, who could easily be bribed. Land was acquired by subterfuge at appreciably higher prices.
Systematic construction was hampered and settlement
could proceed only on a restricted scale.

Most of the public land had been passed on to the
British Mandate Authority by the Turkish administration. The British held it until their authority was
transferred to the United Nations in 1948. When Israel
was founded in the same year, this public land was handed over to the government of Israel.

It included huge tracts of wasteland, desert, and
wilderness which both the Turkish and British governments had been unable to give away to the Arabs, rich or
poor. It also included some tracts of government forest
land. More than half of the land included the Negev, a
trackless desert inhabited only by wandering Bedouins.
This made up what became more than 50% of the total
area of Israel.

Eleven landowners alone possessed over 25,000 acres.
The al—Husseini family owned 50,000 dunams in
various parts of the country. As late as 1922, 750,000
acres of the territory of Palestine mandated to the

British were the property of only 120 Arab families.

The Arab tenant farmers were not displaced by selling their land. While the JNF acquired the majority of its land from absentee landlords of large estates, most of the Arab peasants who sold their land were not dispossessed of their holdings but retained for themselves the more valuable part. The money that the Arabs received enabled them to improve and intensify the cultivation of their remaining estate and derive from it a much better livelihood than before.

For the first time in history the fellaheen could pay off moneylenders and develop their farms. As a result of Jewish settlement, the country became the subject of mass Arab immigration from neighboring, backward countries. Everywhere a Jewish settlement was established, an Arab village followed. Within 25 years of Israel's existence, the Arab population doubled.

The nonpublic land came into the hands of large estate owners due to the poverty of the peasants who constantly had to take up loans to make ends meet until harvest time. Money lenders demanded usurious interest, amounting annually to 40 and 50 per cent and more. The peasants' indebtedness mounted quickly, as the lenders were also the Turkish Government's tax collectors, provided with wide powers to raise sums due and to demand enormous interest on tax arrears. A borrower was not permitted to mortgage his land but was forced to transfer it to the moneylenders. Creditors often allowed peasants to continue working the land as their tenants, demanding half, two-thirds or more of the crop yields as leasehold fees, thus pushing the peasants into a virtual state of serfdom.

Arab families of means exploited the situation to make themselves owners of vast estates which sometimes comprised entire villages. According to a Turkish register dating from the second decade of the 20th century, 144 estate owners possessed a total area of 3,130,000 dunams in Palestine, or an average of 22,000 dunams per family. In the Beer Sheba and Gaza districts alone, there were 28 owners with 2,000,000 dunams to their account.

Much of the land made available to JNF for development and cultivation resulted from the flight of the Arabs following the unexpected rout of the Arab armies of Egypt, Syria, Jordan, Iraq, Saudi Arabia and Lebanon, who had invaded Israel following the Declaration of Independence of Israel on May 14, 1948. Of the 7,990 square miles within the borders of Israel, the Arabs left behind a total of 2,236 square miles, of which 530 square miles was arable land, and the remaining partially tilled or totally barren.

The Arabs were not forced to leave Israel, but did so at their own free will at the urging of their leaders. The Arab exodus had, in fact, begun before the combined assault on Israel, principally by an estimated 20,000 affluent owners of land. The mass of Arabs were exhorted by their leaders to leave and promised that after the Jews were pushed into the sea, they would return to reclaim their land.

One of the great benefits to the Arabs who moved into the territory reclaimed by the JNF was the lifting of their health standards. JNF land reclamation, along with ridding the areas of mosquitoes and other disease-carrying insects, greatly improved the sanitary conditions of the region. The Jews brought with them the knowledge of modern medicine, and opened clinics and hospitals where Arabs were welcomed. Mortality, especially among children, decreased appreciably as the health standards among the Arabs rose.

Joseph Weitz *(1890–1972)* *"father" of 135,000,000 trees, whose practical vision and devotion to the soil in large measure provided the impetus for a major dimension of JNF's contribution to the state.*

Israeli farmers at work in the Negev planting and cultivating the land purchased by JNF funds.

IV
THE JNF SURVIVES THE FIRST WORLD WAR

Between 1908 until the beginning of World War I in 1914, colonization in Palestine took on a new and vigorous growth. The impetus came from a new influx of Russian Jews in the Second Immigration* which had begun in 1904. Young people of all classes began streaming into the country, bringing a new vitality into the JNF settlement operations.

---

* Most of the Second Immigration settlers came from Russia after the programs of the early 1900s. Their aim was to found a new order in Palestine based on socialist principles. With their desire to promote Hebrew as the language of daily life, physical labor as a national duty, and settlement based on the cooperative principle, they laid the foundation for the development of the future Jewish community in Palestine.

By 1914 Jewish agricultural workers and their families totalled some 3,500 persons. They included abut 300 Yemenite Jews, as well as 200 European Jewish women. About half of them were employed in the private villages, and the other half in the JNF settlements that had come into being since 1908.

With the successful initiation of its work in Palestine, the JNF made an appeal to world Jewry, which rallied to its support. As a result, the JNF income rose appreciably and grew with its achievements. By 1907 the JNF income was $338,880. From 1907 to 1911 it increased to $432,000 and in 1913 alone the income was $194,880, an increase of one-third over the previous twelve months. But the advent of war in 1914 clamped a brake on colonizing, and the collection of funds ceased for the duration of the war until 1918.

Palestine in wartime presented a somber picture. The Jewish community, caught in a tragic plight, was not only cut off from its normal resources of supply but was also being harassed by a despotic Turkish governor, Djemal Pasha, the Turkish Commander in Palestine, who suspected the Zionist movement of being hostile to Turkish interests. The Jewish population was continuously under threat of persecution, deportation, and forced evacuation. The Ottoman government mobilized the men for military duty and even confiscated livestock and farm crops. The planters in rural Judea were left trapped by the stoppage of export, since their chief products—wine, oranges, and almonds—were intended for foreign markets. Although the crops of the grain farmers of the Galilee and Samaria were grown for home consumption, distribution was paralyzed. To compound the predicament, the country endured a plague of locusts in 1915 which lasted for three months and totally destroyed all vegetation. To their rescue came funds from abroad, mostly from the Jews of America, who undertook the major financial responsibilities for Palestine throughout the war years.

During the War, the JNF was hard put to preserve its achievements in Palestine. To help meet the crises arising from the cessation of colonizing activities and mounting unemployment, the JNF collected funds to carry out emergency works. The jobless workers were given work on untapped JNF land in removing stones, planting, and carrying out reclamation and drainage projects. Part of the collection was also used to finance vegetable growers who contributed in large measure to supplying the population with food during the years of war and famine. The JNF farms in the Galilee grew wheat and distributed the produce to the Jewish population at moderate prices. Although a number of farms suffered heavily from military requisitioning and destruction in the battle area, most of the settlements, nevertheless, remained intact.

A momentous event in Jewish history occurred on November 2, 1917: the British Government issued the Balfour Declaration* in which it proposed the intention to support the establishment of a national home for the

---

* ..."His Majesty's Government views with favor the establishment in Palestine of a national home for the Jewish people, and will use their best endeavors to facilitate the achievement of this object, it being clearly understood that nothing will be done which may prejudice the civil and religious rights of existing non-Jewish communities in Palestine, or the rights and political status enjoyed by Jews in any other country..."

Jewish people in Palestine. This was followed in 1920 by the British Mandate, in which Britain was awarded control of Palestine as payment for their victories over the Turks in World War I. According to the terms of the Mandate, the area known as Palestine was designated for a Jewish national homeland.

The JNF played a signal role in opening the door to the carrying out of the British Mandate. When the question of the mandate was being considered by the League of Nations, it was the preparatory groundwork carried through by the JNF immediately prior to the War that turned the scales in favor of a home for the Jewish people. Had the Zionists not been able to prove that they were prepared to undertake the responsibilities involved in creating a new nation, it is doubtful that they would have been given an opportunity to establish a national homeland.

In World War I, the *Drang nach Osten* (drive to the East), was the banner under which the Central Powers, Kaiser Wilhelm and his Turkish ally sought control of the crucial area now known as the Middle East. (The term was coined by Winston Churchill.) For the British, control of the region meant free access to India and colonies in Africa.

Thus the land in Palestine purchased by the JNF was in the war's eye of the hurricane. Victory by the Turks would have been followed by depradations, if not the destruction of JNF settlements, pushing the dream of a Jewish homeland back many decades. With the triumph of the Allies in 1919, followed by control of the area under the British Mandate, the program of the Jews to realize statehood became a nearer reality. But British overlordship led to increasing conflict with them and the Arabs.

After World War I, it became an article of faith of Great Britain to resist any outside power, particularly one which would bring Western culture and economic standards in entering the Middle East territories. The Arabs could be kept under exclusive British control only so long as the threat of any intrusion from Western-oriented power was blocked. The Jews with their inexorable drive towards statehood represented the bone that would stick in the British throat. Thus, the implacable English resistance to escaping Jewish immigrants from Europe during World War II.

Menahem Ussishkin *(1863–1941) dominated the JNF scene in Palestine from 1920 to 1941. He was responsible for the purchase of the valuable Jezreel Valley lands, and as Chairman of the Jewish National Fund (1924–1941) extensively increased the area of land acquired by the JNF.*

V

THE PROMISED LAND PURCHASED

The period starting in 1918 and extending through 1936 could be termed "The Conquest of the Valleys," for it saw significant land purchases which included Emek Jezreel, Emek Zevulun, Emek Bet Shean, and Emek Hefer (*Emek* is the Hebrew word for valley). Two of these acquisitions were especially crucial to Israel's future. Emek Jezreel, the largest valley with extensive partly swampy, tracts of land, eventually became the breadbasket of the country. The city of Haifa was extended by the planned development of Emek Zevulun, where suburban land was purchased and made available for healthy growth of the city's population.

Negotiations for the purchase of Jezreel Valley were commenced by Menachem M. Ussishkin* in 1920 with the resources of the JNF.

Opposition among his associates to the high prices demanded by the Arabs for these malaria-infested swamps was overcome by Ussishkin's contention that the inevitable increase in the value of the land would justify the investment. The Jezreel Valley turned out to be one of the JNF's most valuable acquisitions. During the period when Ussishkin served as Chairman of the JNF (1924-1941), the area of land purchased increased from 5,500 acres to 140,250 acres, and the annual income of the JNF increased more than eight times, from 70,000 English pounds to 600,000 English pounds.

Pioneering in a wilderness with sparse funds was achieved at the cost of extreme privation. The occupants of the first settlements in the Emek Jezreel had to face huge swamps covering the area. At immense cost in health and even occasional loss of life from malaria, the settlers managed to drain the Emek Jezreel, located between Nazareth, the Zebulan Valley, Mount Carmel and Gilboa. For years the settlers had no shelter but tents and flimsy wooden huts and were obliged to do heavy physical work with a minimum of nourishing food. As the Emek was a new terrain with no precedent for

---

*Menahem Ussishkin was one of the legendary figures of the country whose personality and insatiable drive dominated the JNF scene during the post-war period from 1920 to 1941. No Jew of Ussishkin's generation was better integrated as a human being, as a Jew and as a Zionist. He will probably go down in the history of the Zionist movement as only next in significance to the founder, Dr. Theodor Herzl. Everything involved in the Zionist goal was his concern: land redemption, immigration and colonization, the organization of the country into a democratically functioning unity, its politics, its self-defense and the education of its youth. What was named the Foundation for Israel in the United States by the author, was originally the Ussishkin League.

cultivation, the growth of crops succeeded only after much experimentation with the earth. Eventually, irrigation plants were installed and roads built in the area.

Most of the incoming settlers after 1920 had to secure contracts from the mandatory government for roads, railways, bridges, and other public works. The story of these young road builders is one of fierce toil under a subtropical sun, of malarial fever and numerous hardships. Other pioneers found work in the plantation villages, the kibbutzim, or were employed on the drainage and afforestation works of the JNF.

The Emek Jezreel was followed by other purchases of large tracts in Emek Zevulun, Emek Hepher, and the Jordan Valley, laying the foundation for a continous area of Jewish settlement from Haifa to Lake Tiberias, designed to extablish a network of related farming areas thoughout the country.

The enemies of the settlers were not confined to malaria, tropical sun and rocky terrain. In April 1936 the Arabs in Jaffa launched riots which rapidly spread throughout the country. It was in those years that the JNF acquired the Menashe Hills, the Western Galilee, and the area of the Huleh Valley.

In the face of incessant attacks by organized Arab bands, the buying of land had to be followed by immediate settlement which acted as a barrier to assault. This led to a new form of colonization known as the Tower and Stockade. In the dead of night, a group of settlers would leave in trucks loaded with a pre-fabricated watchtower and huts, proceed speedily through hostile neighborhoods, put up temporary buildings, erect a barbed wire fence and await the inevitable attack by the

Arabs. Water was lacking, supplies could not be brought up. While fortifications were inadequate, reinforcements were often completely cut off. But by sheer willpower and courage, the few were able to withstand the many, and amazingly a new settlement was born.

Just before the outbreak of war in 1939, the British government published its infamous White Paper ending almost all legal immigration into Palestine and restricting land purchases by Jews to a bare 5% of the country. The White Paper asserted that the Balfour Declaration had not envisaged the conversion of all Palestine into a Jewish State but merely the establishment in the country of "a Jewish National Home," which meant the development of Palestine's existing Jewish community (450,000 or almost one-third of the total population) into a center for the Jewish people. In order to allay the Arabs' fear of continued immigration leading to a Jewish majority in the country, the White Paper limited the admission of Jews to only 75,000 in subsequent years. This would bring the Jewish population to about one-third of Palestine's total population, after which no Jewish immigration would be permitted without the agreement of the Arabs. Moreover, in order to prevent Arabs from becoming landless, restrictions were to be imposed on land transfers to Jews. The nefarious White Paper forbade all land purchase by Jews in 60% of Palestine, restricted it severely in another 35%, and permitted the Jews to buy land only in 5% of the area.

Immediately upon its publication, the White Paper was severely denounced by the Jews as a breach of faith with the Jewish people. It left Palestine Jewry at the mercy of the Arab majority and closed the country to Jews now fleeing Nazi persecution.

The Jews fought back. The very law which barred most of the soil to the Jews acted as a spur for the Jewish National Fund to intensify its acquisition efforts. What was characterized as "almost impossible" was done to extend Jewish holdings in Palestine during this period. Using such devices as legal loopholes and financial, legal and personal risks, including underground contact with Arabs, the JNF was able to acquire half a million dunams and establish 139 new villages. Mostly border settlements, they later also served as defense posts.

In 1942, the World Zionist Organization demanded the replacement of the British by a Jewish State with unrestricted Jewish immigration. An Anglo-American Committee of Inquiry report in 1946 rejected the idea of the partition of Palestine into an Arab and Jewish state and recommended instead a binational state under continuing British control, with the immediate admission of 100,000 Jews and an end to land purchase restrictions imposed in 1940. None of these proposals was ever fully implemented.

After the second World War, in spite of the JNF purchase of numerous tracts of the vast Negev desert, the British were determined to keep it under their control. Since there was only sparse settlement in the area, the holdings had to be populated immediately if the Jews were to have any real claim to the region. The British threatened to oppose by force any attempts at Jewish settlement. But on the day after Yom Kippur, 1946, hundreds of young settlers penetrated the Negev, which came as a complete surprise to the British and Arabs. In one night eleven settlements were established on JNF land. The Jews were in the Negev to stay.

From 1939 to 1947, the most important area of land purchase was in Southern Palestine. In this period the JNF acquired 22,750 acres in the Negev, and 18,750 acres in the Judean Plain. The Galilee occupied the second place in acquisition of land. The holdings of the JNF more than tripled during that period. New areas were acquired in both the mountainous western part of the country and in the Huleh Valley.

A plan submitted by the United Nations Special Committee on Palestine recommending that Palestine be partitioned into separate and independent Arab and Jewish states was approved by the General Assembly of the United Nations on November 29, 1947. The JNF policy of buying land in strategic areas helped determine the borders of the future Jewish State. When earlier the Palestine Fact-Finding Commission of UNSCOP took up its work in 1947, new outpost settlements on JNF land were already in existence in many parts of the country, from the Galilee and the Huleh Valley in the north to the Beersheba region of the Negev in the south. The results were that the borders proposed by the Commission for the future Jewish State in large measure tended to include outlying Jewish villages and undeveloped land property. In the United Nations' decision of November, 1947 to partition Palestine, those boundaries were followed for the establishment of a Jewish State, which was proclaimed on May 14, 1948.

On the following day the armies of Lebanon and Syria in the North, Jordan in the East, and Egypt in the South flouted the U.N. decision and attacked the fledgling Jewish State. The Jewish farmers in the agricultural settlements at the borders held out with supreme courage and self-sacrifice against overwhelming odds, and repulsed the enemy. The strategic location of the Jewish settlements had become a decisive factor in the victory of the War of Independence.

First trees of an American Forest in Memory of Nameless Martyrs planted in a ceremony in the Judean Hills by Ira Hirschmann and American Ambassador Monnett B. Davis on November 8, 1951. A commemorative scroll by the JNF was presented to Mr. Hirschmann as a tribute to his rescue work. Present were representatives of thousands of Jews from the Balkans who were saved.

VI

POST-WAR ISRAEL: JNF EXPANDS

With the establishment of the State of Israel, vast areas were abandoned by Arabs who fled from Israel during the War of Independence. Their farms and fields could not be allowed to lie fallow. They had to be cultivated to provide for hundreds of new Jewish immigrants. There were, in addition, thousands of acres which had lain waste for centuries, particularly in the hilly areas. The JNF stood ready to assume responsibility for these abandoned lands. The Israel government therefore transferred state lands to the JNF in 1949 and 1950 which could be cultivated or made useful for farming through reclamation, thus doubling the total of JNF property in the first years of statehood.

The function of the JNF now shifted in emphasis from land purchase to land reclamation and development. Little of the area of the State of Israel was under cultivation when it came into being; the greatest part was still

unfit for use. In the first decade since the founding of
the State, the JNF converted hundreds of thousands of
acres of rock and stone into areas of soil. In this period it
reclaimed 62,500 acres of desolate land for agricultural
use, drained and dried 65,000 acres of marshland, revived 37,500 acres of mountain, sand and wadis by planting
40 million trees, and laid 435 miles of roads and paths in
the mountains. The meaning of these statistics can only
be evaluated in terms of the labor and valor of people
dedicated to sow its ardent future.

With this major acquisiton of acreage, it became
apparent that the lands of Israel were, in effect, mainly
concentrated in the hands of two principal owners; the
State and the Jewish National Fund. The State, through
the Agricultural Department and the JNF, were both involved in the same aspects of land management: leasing,
exploration, reclamation, afforestation, and development. This parallel activity created problems which called for a solution for the elimination of duplication and
waste.

In 1960 the Israeli Knesset passed the Land Authority
Bill giving the JNF the exclusive right to land reclamation, land development, and afforestation for the entire
territory of the State of Israel. Another triumph was
scored by the JNF with the acceptance and extension of
the basic principle that the land acquired by it belongs to
all Jewish people and shall never be sold. This Biblical
injunction, long the keystone of JNF policy, was now
established as the guiding principle for all collectively
held land in Israel: about 90 per cent of the territory of
the State. A new era for the JNF was inaugurated.

Under the Land Authority Act, all public lands,

whether owned by the State or constituting property of the JNF, were pooled for the purpose of administration and reclamation. Two central authorities were organized to manage the land: The Land Administration Authority and the Land Development Authority.

The Land Administration Authority administered all national land domains, including the determination of the policy of zoning, town and village planning, urban and agricultural settlement, and the leasing of land to settlers.

The second authority entrusted to the JNF the responsibility for soil improvement, land development, and afforestation for all national land. The wastelands constituting 75 per cent of the surface of Israel — all the rocky hillsides, sand dunes, the other desert areas and swamps were waiting to be transformed into farms, towns, and woodlands. Thus the JNF became the exclusive arm for all land develpment in Israel.

Through the creation of the Land Authority, the State of Israel posed a magnificent challenge to the Jewish National Fund to launch a huge offensive against desolation and to enrich the physical and economic resources of the State. On another level, it not only expanded the scope of the JNF, but recharged its spirit. It was hailed as the beginning of a new chapter, not only in the history of the Fund, but also in the annals of the upbuilding of the Jewish State.

Since then, achievements were fulfilled in all aspects of land development. Soil was prepared for agriculture; for homes in outlying areas, for rural industries, and development towns. Forests were planted for ecology, to halt erosion, to fertilize the desert, for relaxaton, and for the beauty of the land. Roads were cut through desolate regions, border areas, and difficult mountain terrain. The organization was proving worthy of its heritage and its newly entrusted goals.

JNF worker preparing the land for settlement by dislodging giant rocks by hand. Before the advent of tractors and bulldozers, all the undeveloped land had to be cleared by the use of manual labor, a back-breaking task.

VII
CREATING
THE SETTLEMENTS

An immediate task facing the State following its in-auguration in 1948 was the settling of the waves of mass immigration. To speed up the process, the JNF devised temporary "work villages" where settlers in the initial years earned their livelihood as hired laborers of the organization. As an example, villages were set up in a critical area in the hills of Judea. This provided new immigrants with a place to live and work on the rocky terrain and terraces cleared by JNF for the settlers to plant forests. The living quarters, which were hastily set up, had only limited and rugged housing facilities.

But these were temporary. Today settlements with more attractive housing and convenient facilities have been created by a cooperative effort of the JNF and other settlement authorities* who have succeeded in making them sound, inviting living quarters.

This is the fulfillment of a successful formula for the planning of each settlement. The 'anatomy' of settlements offers an interesting and instructive pattern of the indispensible use of the JNF experience:

It begins with the general location for a settlement proposed by the Jewish Agency. Whether it will be a kibbutz, moshav, or industrial center is determined by the nature of the terrain. After a blueprint is drawn up, an overall architectural plan is outlined with the location of each house in relation to farming units and proximity to roads.

The JNF now takes over the planning and preparation of the project. First examining the site to determine costs, the Fund draws up a working program to prepare the land for settlement including time schedules and types of machinery to be used. The JNF engineering teams carry out the major primary steps, leveling the land with trucks, tractors, and bulldozers. Only then does the Ministry of Housing take over to construct actual living quarters and farming installations.

The problems in the creation of new settlements vary throughout the country. No area is alike, each having its special problems of terrain. The soil is often poor, demanding costly labor to fertilize it; the sparseness of water requires expensive pipe and plumbing installations; extensive work in building a network of roads is needed to reach the settlements.

---

* Israel Land Authority, Department of Settlement and Architecture of the Jewish Agency, and Ministry of Housing.

One of the most dramatic examples of overcoming prodigious problems with the application of the JNF planning techniques is in the Arava where 13 settlements have been created in barren desert region stretching for 115 miles along Jordan's border from the southern tip of the Dead Sea to the port of Eilat on the Red Sea in the eastern part of the Negev. A desert timeless and endless, part of the former region of Sodom and Gemorrah, the Arava possesses the dubious distinction of being the driest and the lowest expanse on the face of the earth. With the Kingdom of Jordan immediately to the east, the Arava is Israel's longest continuous frontier and has become the central artery connecting the heart of the country with the Red Sea, through which all maritime trade to the east and the south must pass.

The climate is the severest problem. With 350 days of sun each year and the temperature above 100 degrees much of the time, the Arava is a virtual blast furnace of fiery heat and swirling red sands. The less than two inches of annual rain comes as a down-pour and floods the land with millions of cubic feet of water accompanied by tons of pebbles which inundate the soil, much of which is too salty for cultivation without the use of fertilizers.

With the exception of a few Bedouin caravans, the Arava was abandoned and empty from the seventh century until the area became part of the State of Israel in 1949, when the first farming efforts in the region were initiated. Only after much trial and error the Arava began to yield to the hand of the young Jewish settlers. Now the warm winters permit the growing of fruits, vegetables, and flowers year round, which can be exported to Europe where they arrive at a time when the are in short supply.

Today the caravan route of old is being turned into a highway of JNF construction. Rising out of the desert, the thirteen settlements are oases of life, truly man-made miracles. Neat houses now dot the horizon, surronded with green gardens, date and other fruit plantations, fields made ready for their crops, and sprinklers slaking the thirst of the soil. The struggle of man to awaken the soil from the slumber of centuries has resulted in an imperishable achievement of the JNF in creating a fertile land to welcome the new settlers of the region.

One of the most successful settlements in the Arava is Moshav Hatzeva, located just south of the Dead Sea at the beginning of the Arava Valley in the region known as the Great Syria-African Rift. It is desert terrain with thorny shrubs and an occasional stunted acacia tree decorating the rolling dunes, with a landscape not dissimilar to that of the state of Arizona. The climate is arid, with temperatures reaching 110-115 degrees between the end of July and the middle of September. During the spring months, sand-storms sweep across the area, propelled by howling winds.

Hatzeva was originally founded as an outpost of the Nahal* (Army Pioneer Settlers Corps) in 1965. Two years later, prefabricated houses were built and the moshav was provided with a dining room and cooperatively worked fields. It was not until 1970 that

---

* Nahal units combine soldiering with pioneering. After a few months' intensive military training, groups are assigned for nearly a year to villages where they receive on the job instruction in agriculture. A group of men and women join a frontier outpost or set up a new one of their own, often in areas as yet too insecure or difficult for normal civilian habitation.

the moshav's first 20 houses were completed for the members to move in with their tractors and their meager possessions.

The area has since been the site of an extensive JNF land reclamation project where some 625 acres have already been made available. Preparation of the site of Hatzeva had to meet the challenge of the desert's all-encroaching sands. First the fields were levelled and destoned for the rich topsoil brought in by truck. The JNF workers then transplanted date palms and desert shrubbery at the site to improve the landscaping of the residential area.

Today, Hatzeva is principally engaged in market farming. The season is short, from November to April, demanding intensive work during the limited period. The farmers grow melons, cucumbers, squashes, tomatoes, peppers, eggplants, and onions. Recently, flowers have been grown for export to Holland, and a date plantation is currently producing its first crops.

Upon becoming a full member of the Moshav after being interviewed for acceptance, each family receives a standard house of three bedrooms, a living room, kitchen, bathroom, and bomb shelter. As new settlers they are given all the basic needs to start farming, including a tractor, irrigation systems, the use of the Moshav's common agricultural equipment and an initial six acres of land to grow his crops. The newcomer is not provided with these essentials free of cost. The tractor itself amounts to some 40,000 pounds, but each family is given a start by the Moshav with loans on easy terms. Most families pay off their debts within five years.

Hatzeva, laid out like a mosaic on the vast desert floor constitutes a virtual model of the successful Israeli

melting pot. Here is an example of Jewish immigrants
from all walks of life and countries forming a natural,
fully integrated and inseparable bond to build a common
future, foregoing another link along the far-flung desert
waste and at the same time providing a military rampart
on the Jordanian frontier.

Another thriving moshav in the Arava is Neot
Hakikar, located at the southern tip of the Dead Sea
depression on the dried out salt basin known as the
Sodom Plains, near the Sodom-Arava Road. Biblically,
the Sodom Plains — cracked open by the scorching sun
and swept away by the lightning floods — was one of the
most inhospitable places, originally settled by the
Children of Israel. These were the lands ascribed in the
Bible as having been given by God to Lot, watered by
the fresh water spring of Kikar.

In 1902 Neot Hakikar had its modest beginnings as a
cattle ranch. Six years later steps were taken to
organize the site as an agricultural settlement but
because of hostile conditions, early settlement was stopped.

Neot Hakikar was first established as a collective
moshav in 1971. Prior to this, some 650 acres of land had
been reclaimed by the JNF and a road had been created
from the Arava Highway to the present site of the
moshav. This was made possible from the contributions
raised by the South African and Australian Jewish communities in the early 1960s. Neot Hakikar's farmers are
evenly divided between former members of kibbutzim
and moshavim, former city dwellers, and new immigrants. No previous agricultural experience is required
and they adapt equally well to the physical conditions of
farming life.

It is, however, still in the first stages of development. Today the moshav numbers 45 families and there are virtually no "drop-outs". New, three-bedroomed houses are being constructed on land reclaimed by the JNF to enable the admission of the five to ten families that are accepted for membership each year.

Life is hard on the moshav. Working physically under the relentless sun during the summer months, according to one of the members, "one gets used to the heat and the sweat. It is the physical isolation that imposes a greater hardship upon the settlers." These idealistic pioneers, many of them coming from big towns, are now cut off from cultural centers and the comforts of civilization.

Meanwhile, Neot Hakikar continues to expand its production, absorb new families and invest resources in the new primary school that it has opened and the supermarket it runs at local expense to the moshav. The settlers are optimistic about the future, in spite of the isolation and the harsh conditions they must face in order to exist.

There is no substitute for the security that is provided by villages, settlements, and towns set up along the borders of the country. Settlers guard their homes, work their fields and help build communities in areas that would otherwise lay exposed as open invitations for terrorists to find hiding places when crossing the borders. The towns along the borders transform desolate paths into busy thoroughfares that serve as barriers to deter and prevent the infiltration of invaders.

But all border settlements are not immune to the sneak attacks of the Arabs. Along the Lebanon frontier the Israelies are regular targets for PLO guns.

Residents and children of Kiryat Shemona, Ma'alot, and Shelomi have been the victims of vicious assaults. In 1974 in Ma'alot a school was attacked in which 18 Israeli children were killed and more than 70 injured. The settlers on this front have in effect become front line soldiers in their everyday lives, obliged to face the terrorist attacks which are unrelenting.

Nevertheless, efforts are made by the JNF to make day-to-day living as normal and agreeable as possible. The presence of the trenches and shelters along the streets is minimized. The sandbags around the houses are hidden by greenery, children have space in which to play, and recreation areas are provided with pleasant surroundings for relaxation and escape from the tensions of border life.

No area could have appeared more remote and impractical for settlement than the village of Yamit in the Sinai desert. Established on July 28, 1973, it is located on the shores of the Mediterranean Sea between Rafah and El Arish in the north, eight miles from the former Israeli border in the sands below steep mountains separating the Mediterranean from the desert. The JNF arrived on the site first to help plan and survey the immense problems and determine if they could be overcome for the settlement to become a reality. To do so, they had to cope with sand dunes that changed with the slightest wind, bringing about an undulating land surface unsuitable for planting. JNF workers first flattened the terrain by shaving off the hills and filling in the valleys until the area was flat; a stupendous task. Over one million, 400 cubic meters of sand were moved by the JNF in reclaiming 1,200 dunams for Yamit.

The Ministry of Housing then speedily put up seven units of prefabricated homes of one and two stories, complete with electricity and other facilities in the midst of the desert dunes. The houses, like the sand dunes, looked as if they might fly away with the first sandstorm. But the JNF workers managed to control the sand from floating loose by planting 200 acacia and tamarisk trees in a tight circle around the settlement.

The acreage was purchased for large sums from the nomadic Bedouins. Besides payment for each dunam, additional sums were required for each palm tree. The Bedouins have insisted on remaining there while the Israelis grow their tomatoes, squash and delicious dates from the palms, the unofficial trademark of Yamit. The palms were brought by the JNF from El Arish in the Negev and replanted there.

With about 500 inhabitants, Yamit's main occupation is farming. It is a town created especially for its people, landscaped for recreational activities with its scenic beach just meters away where paths between the palm trees lead to picnic tables and other camping facilities. The fresh sea air in a desert landscape makes Yamit a relatively pleasant place to live in spite of its remoteness from any civilized town, and proximity to its neighbor, Egypt.*

---

* Author's note: On a visit to Israel in the Spring of 1978, I rode through the desert heat to Yamit where I visited the modest, almost clinically clean farm home of Ramy and Rachel Oved, aged 30 and 27.

Originally from Yemen without any background in farming, they had graduated from the Israel Agricultural School. They volunteered to settle in the desert away from the amenities of civilization and enjoy "making a living" but also feeling that "we are soldiers on the front row facing the Arabs."

Here, surrounded by an oasis of sand, I witnessed the growth of a bounty of incredibly beautiful flowers. Giant chrysanthemums, gladiolas and roses seemed almost unreal. Ramy had developed a simple machine about two feet in height which distributed precious water and fertilizer simultaneously via separate tubes to the roots of flowers in minimal quantities. It worked by computer and could be controlled from the farmer's house.

How incredible it seemed that this opulent growth destined for the expensive florists in major cities of the U.S. should originate in the sands of the deserts a few miles from Gaza on the border of Egypt.

I asked this handsome couple about their plans for the future. "All future plans are frozen," they answered, due to the unsettled political situation. They did confess a degree of concern, but only for Israel's safety, not their own. In spite of exertions that had gone into the creation of their home and expanding farm, they volunteered, "If it would help to bring peace to Israel, we would gladly move and begin again elsewhere."

VIII
PUSHING BACK THE DESERT

In its drive to reclaim the land, the JNF was obliged to cope with soil so resistant that it literally fought back. The incrustation resulting from centuries of neglect seemed to act as a defiance against efforts to fertilize and cultivate it. One of the major obstacles was erosion. This was made more acute by the fact that Israel is mostly hilly country. Hills occupy most of the country west of the Jordan, in the Negev and in the northern half of the country. To prepare these hill regions for farming, a relentless war had to be fought against the corroded soil brought about principally by wind, sun, and rain. During the long dry summer months most of the natural vegetation withered and could not hold the soil which had crumbled under the blistering sun. The heavy

showers that came with the first autumn rains swept the
loosened dry soil away from the steep hillsides. Even the
rocky underpinnings on the many slopes in Judea and
the Galilee were laid bare by erosion.

The solution was found in contour plowing and terracing, which was carried out by removing loose stones
from surface slopes and blasting out the deeply sunk
rocks which hindered plowing. This was followed by terracing, which meant reshaping the curved slopes into
flat-surfaced banks of soil supported by piles of stones.
The sides of the hills which had defied access for plowing, now became a series of landscaped fertile steps of
soil for farming. This acomplishment was all the more
remarkable since there were no adequate tools and
equipment for the rugged labor it demanded. In the early stages some of the settlers were obliged to dislodge
the giant boulders and fill the holes with their bare
hands.

It was in the northern Negev that the resistant soil offered the greatest challenge. Here sudden flash floods
opened deep, zig-zagging gulleys in the loose soil and
bulldozers were needed to close up the ravines. To serve
as windbreaks, the JNF planted thousands of trees in
rows which prevented sand storms from creating dunes,
and nurtured the soil to save it from being parched by
the hot dry winds.

It was the salt in the soil which deterred the growth of
vegetation in much of the desert. The problem of revi-
talizing the soil was met by the JNF through the
resourceful creation of a method called rinsing. It was a
process that worked by flooding the surfaces of the
earth with water which quickly percolated into the

ground, dissolving the salts below the plant roots where they could not be damaged. Thanks to the initiation of this system, former desert areas were transformed into fertility and have produced first-grade fruit, flowers, and vegetables for export.

While the soil adjacent to the Mediterranean shores was good it was menaced by shifting sand dunes covering Israel's coast which encroached and gradually overran the fertile soil, burying it under a blanket of worthless sand. This sandy sweep of the dunes was arrested by the planting of eucalyptus and tamerisk trees in rows along borders.

The menace of the shifting sand dunes and how it was overcome is described in a booklet published on the anniversary of the founding of Rishon le Zion, a settlement along the coast of the Mediterannean Sea. The farmers had planted fruit trees, almonds, and figs, and after a few years they were alarmed to see the advancing hills of sand surround the trees and threaten them on all sides. Advised by the JNF to plant large numbers of trees along the edge of the dunes to form a green wall of defense to prevent the sand's further advance, they built a living fence of eucalyptus trees along the perimeter of the dunes to anchor the sands. The waves of sand were halted.

Water: the Critical Shortage

Added to the barriers in pushing the desert back was the acute shortage of water suffered by the entire area. Half of Israel is desert (the Negev) which receives less than 7 inches of rainfall per year. Israel's southern seaport, Eilat, has an annual rainfall of only 1.2 inches. Even the capital, Jerusalem is on the edge of the Judean handicapped by the irregularity of precipitation. The rainy season lasts, at most, for several months, but during the whole summer not a single drop of rain may be expected.

The settlers managed to overcome this critical water shortage by first adopting the ancient method of collecting rainwater through cisterns built in the ground, a primitive means widely used around mountain villages and towns. Secondly, water was retained in large dams which arrested the flow of heavy rains down mountain sides. The water was then transferred to settlements through iron pipes constructed by the JNF.*

But it was the insidious malarial swamps that became the worst and direst threat to settlement work and life itself. In the settlement of Hadera in the central coastal plain, for example, the population was decimated by malaria. People arrived and disappeared so rapidly that at times the survivors lost count and did not know whose funeral they were attending. Still, the remaining settlers at Hadera, realizing that sadness and despair were the companions of malaria and death, refused to succumb. They stayed and continued to fight malaria with quinine (and an occasional swallow of cognac to lift up their spirits).

The JNF met the problem through swamp drainage. Ditches were excavated and placed like ribbons throughout the swamp area, causing the water from the

---

*Today, by creation of the National Water Carrier System, the Government of Israel has been able to transfer water from regions in the country with plenty to areas of scarcity. This has permitted an increase of the area under irrigation from 75,000 acres in 1948 to 440,000 acres today. Water is pumped up from Lake Kinneret and flows through an 108 inch diameter pipeline along the Mediterannean coastal plain to the Negev, where it irrigates vast tracts of desert.

swamp to run down the ditches to a lower level. It was then removed from the marsh where the ground water table was lowered by systems of subterranean clay pipes or narrow surface trenches. The remaining water was used up by the planting of eucalyptus trees. Thanks to this original means of drainage, fetid wastes were transformed into farmland. The valleys of Jezreel, Hefer, Bet Shean, and Zebulun (Haifa Bay) were examples of the use of this system and are today the most flourishing parts of the country.

The most dramatic and prodigious achievement resulting from swamp drainage was in the Huleh Valley. The cleansing and transformation by 1957 of this 45,000 acre stagnating lake (adjacent to Syria) from an almost hopeless infested swamp to the richest farmland in the country has resulted in one of Israel's most priceless assets. The Huleh Valley is but a small section of the giant Syrian-East African Rift, one of the deepest scars in the rock crust of the earth. Of the numerous animals of the lake and swamps, one of the smallest proved decisive for the fate of man in the valley — the anapholes mosquito, which by its sting spreads malaria. Consequently, the valley was only thinly inhabited in the past, and the dread disease was endemic among the primitive villagers who derived their meager existence from tending water buffaloes and preparing reed mats. The first Jewish settlers in the area also suffered painfully from malaria.

In 1934, the JNF acquired the Huleh Concession from Syrian landlords for draining the lake and swamps and bought land in the center and north of the Valley. More Jewish settlements came into being. Detailed plans for the drainage were prepared, but could be carried out by the JNF only after statehood was achieved, in the years 1950-1957.

The JNF deepened and widened an outlet from the Huleh Basin southwards into Lake Kinneret to lower the water level and constructed three canals which permitted a strong flow to empty the lake and swamps of their waters. Fifteen thousand acres of highly fertile peat soil, hidden from time immemorial beneath the papyrus jungle, could for the first time be plowed and sown. The rich bog of earth provided a quality of soil unmatched by any in the region, which soon gave record yields of maize, cotton, ground nuts, and flower bulbs. The sponge-like peat soil has proved to be especially desirable for the cultivation of rice. The Huleh also serves as an essential military rampart against Syria. Its reclamation has opened the way for the establishment of many new agricultural settlements on the vulnerable northeast frontier where Israel has common borders with Syria and Lebanon. The architect of this miracle of construction was an engineering genius from Chicago, J.R. Sensibar, who was dedicated to the JNF.

In early 1950 when any consideration of draining the Huleh seemed remote, the writer while touring the area with Sensibar, witnessed wild boars running through the swamp. The animals were not the only obstacles encountered, as we were obliged to take cover from a barrage of bullets from nearby Syrian hills. The Syrian Government made numerous attempts to hâlt the work. JNF workers were fired upon and some were killed. Although the Syrians caused numerous and expensive delays, they could not halt the project. Its re-creation from a wasted bog into a precious gem in Israel's agricultural crown, is living testimony to JNF resourcefulness and tenacity.

View of the developed Huleh Valley, the most dramatic and prodigious achievement in Israel resulting from swamp drainage. the cleansing and transformation by 1957 of this 45,000 acre stagnating lake (adjacent to Syria) from an almost hopeless infested swamp to the richest farmland in the country has resulted in one of Israel's most priceless assets.

Terracing in the Judean Hills, a method used to counteract erosion by reshaping the curved slopes into flat-surfaced banks of soil supported by piles of stones. The sides of myriad hills which had defied access for plowing, have been transformed into a vast series of landscaped fertile steps of soil for farming.

IX

GREEN MANSIONS
IN THE SKIES

No single conception of the JNF proved more vital for the future development of the nation than its stupendous tree-planting program. Begun with individual seed planting and carried out on an increasing scale, it multiplied into forests that transformed the landscape of the country, while adding to the fertility of the soil and serving as an essential barrier against enemy invasion.

The JNF operations extended from land purchasing to land development, agricultural experimentation, and planting of forests. In no small measure, this giant revolutionary step owes its impetus to the practical vision of one man: Joseph Weitz. Weitz' fanatical devotion to the soil, with his unbounded energy and zeal, succeeded in adding a major essential dimension to the State.

"Joseph Weitz, a short, wiry agronomist with steel-springs for legs led me through rocky fields and up steep slopes to admire some of his 'children.' To him the growing of green things was a religion. We would cross a field lush with wheat, and he would point out that not long ago this had been a swamp where malaria had taken the lives of many pioneers... Weitz spoke of the fifty million trees that had been planted by that time (1945) and the two hundred million more that would be put into the soil in next decade".*

It was David Ben-Gurion who had told the writer before the establishment of the State that one of his deepest concerns was that uninterrupted acres of desert sand served as an open invitation to enemy invasion. Forests of trees would constitute a bulwark for the defense of the new nation under siege.

When the State was established in 1948, five million trees had been planted. By 1978, the number had grown to 135 million, and at the present rate may reach the second 100 million mark by the end of the century.

Forests held a prominent place in the Israel of Biblical times. Before Moses led the children of Israel into the Promised Land, the mountains of upper and lower Galilee were said to be alive with magnificent forests of cypress and beech. Further north, in Lebanon, tall cedars rose from the slopes, and all of Samaria was wooded. Saul, the first king of Israel, battled the Philistines in a forest, and David slew Goliath in the Valley of the Pistachio Tree. The tragic death of David's

---

Caution to the Winds, David McKay, 1962

beloved son, Absalom, took place in a battle which the author of the Book of Samuel describes as follows: "For the battle was there scattered over the face of all the country, and the wood devoured more people that day than the sword devoured." Absalom met his death "under the thick boughs of a great oak" when his hair became entangled in its branches.

Biblical name-places recall forests and woods. The stretch from Sha'ar Hagai to Motza was called "Mount of the Forest," and Abu Gosh was known in ancient times as "City of the Forests."

As late as the twelfth century, the area known as Palestine was heavily wooded. Dr. Hans Prutz, an authority on the Crusades, wrote in 1883:

"Today the forests of Syria and Palestine appear sparse in comparison with former times when most of the hills were wooded. The shores of the Sea of Galilee were covered with trees, the slopes of Mt. Tabor were under forest, and the Judean hills as far as Jerusalem and the Hebron hills, which today are almost bare, then supplied the inhabitants of Jerusalem with all the wood they needed."

In the ensuing centuries, complete devastation over-took the forests. The first Jewish pioneers in the 19th century found a harsh, desolate country bare of trees under the pitiless sun. The destruction began with the Bedouin herdsmen and their flocks. Black goats, nibbling away at the young shoots and bark of trees, hastened their degeneration into lowly scrub. Trees were felled by shepherds for firewood and nomads deliberately burned down forests to make room for grazing land.

An early Jewish purchaser of land described the desolate treeless condition of Beersheba in 1911:

> "The whole region, with its hills and ravines is one large wilderness, and most of the terrain is criss-crossed by dry water courses (wadis). No matter where you turn there is neither village nor any kind of permanent human habitation; not a tree in sight nor any hint of cultivated plant—only the black tents of the Bedouins and their camels and herds of goats. Water there is none, not in streams nor in wells, and the earth is hard and arid."

Today the city of Beersheba is the fifth city in population in Israel, a thriving community that had its roots in the JNF cultivation of its soil.

The thorough demolition of forests was a by-product of the many wars fought in the area. Roman legions were experts in felling entire woodlands for use in fortifying their camps, which was repeated time and again in the many wars that followed.

The Turks, lacking coal for their steam engines in the First World War and needing major supplies of wood for railroad ties, cut down extensive forests, choosing the stoutest branches and trunks to fell.

Extensive forests became a key project of the JNF in the inherent improvement of the nation. The scorched ground, robbed of its forest cover, acted as a serious brake against the development of the country. Only trees could protect the soil. It was the forests in the hills that prevented the topsoil from being washed away by the winter rains. In the Negev, trees were planted to anchor the shifting sand dunes while avenues of trees sheltered the crops from desert storms. Added to this were the many other assets provided by forests, their essential wood, their role in beautifying Israel's landscape, and the improvement of the environment as well as their contribution to the nation's security.

The basis for forestry legislation in Israel was derived from British law. It was the Palestine Forest Ordinance of 1926 which may be regarded as the first legislation in Palestine, and possibly in the whole of the Middle East, based on the premise that natural woodland should no longer be outside the law's domain and that new forest trees should be planted. Predating the founding of modern Israel by more than 20 years, it provided both framework and precedent for progressive legislation in the new state extending the necessary protection of forests and trees.

The start of afforestation in Palestine began in 1910 when an olive grove — the Herzl Forest — was planted at Ben-Shemen, east of Tel Aviv. In the next few years similar plantings were started, financed by European and Central European Jews. But it took ten years to learn that a costly mistake had been made. While olive trees flourished in the valleys and lower slopes, they did not grow well in the mountains. The high ground was better suited to such needle-bearing trees as pines, acacias, and casuarinas.

Another lesson was learned in 1920 when an attempt was made to plant stone pines, brought from Lebanon. The tops of this species soon yellowed, and whole trees turned sickly and died. Two years later they were replaced by native Jerusalem pines, which have flourished in all mountainous areas.

In 1924 the first large-scale JNF afforestation project was begun with the planting of the Balfour Forest in northern Palestine, honoring the British statesman who helped restore that country to its people. This time British and American Jews were the major contributors. Some 5,000,000 trees have since been planted in this forest.

In 1948, when Israel became a nation, JNF forests served a vital purpose in providing employment for tens of thousands of new immigrants who were streaming into the country from the four corners of the earth. Many of the new settlers were city dwellers and it was difficult to convert them into farmers overnight. The newcomers were put to work planting trees and maintaining the forests. Many adults and even elderly people who had never done any physical work, especially farm work, now learned to hold a hoe and a mattock, to dig pits, clear weeds, and plant trees.

The centuries of neglect were not the only "enemies" the JNF workers had to overcome. The Arabs mounted relentless attacks on the settlers in their desparate effort to halt the afforestation progress. Joseph Weitz, describes how the Hulda forest suffered a disaster during the "disturbances" of the summer of 1929, when Jewish lives and property came under violent attack from the rampaging Arabs:

"One night the Arabs descended on Hulda and maliciously set fire to the forest. Next day, I myself saw its smoke and ashes. The scorched and blackened trees had been stripped, and only the uppermost cluster of charred pine needles still moved desolately in their orphanhood. This was my first forest fire, and I was left shaken and inconsolable. All through the autumn months I did not return to Hulda, but a month after the first rain I stopped by to see if there was anything to be done to restore the burnt forest. On entering the wood I halted in amazement at the sight which greeted me. The green floor of the forest was one huge seedbed of myriads of tiny pines growing together in close array, each keeping joyful company with its neighbor."*

And with its long, dry summer season, forest fires are another ever-present menace to Israel. Hoeing and ploughing dry weeds act as a deterrent to the spread of flames. But the major resistance to conflagrations was in the creation of networks of watch towers which Israel has built in the center of forest areas as a decisive step in fire prevention. Guards are posted on those towers from dawn to sunset during the summer months to trace smoke of fires that have begun. These guards are in radio-telephone contact with motorized patrols of forest workers who can reach endangered site in a matter of minutes. The use of chemicals as fire deterrents are particularly important in fighting forest fires as only relatively small water tankers can be brought up to outlying sites.

In a span of thirty years the JNF has added 135,000 acres of trees to the afforested area of Israel, from 25,000 acres in 1948 to more than 160,000 in 1978. Most of the forest was on arid, hilly, or mountainous land that had been recovered with the rest in the valleys. Mt.

---

*Joseph Weitz, *Forests and Afforestation in Israel,* Massada Press, Jerusalem, 1974, p. 57

Carmel, the Nazareth Hills, the Manassah Hills, the Saf-
ed Hills, the Judean foothills, the eastern Jezreel Valley,
and the western Galilee all pay tribute to the vision of
JNF.

The planting of verdant wood in the midst of the
Negev desert was another resourceful step by the JNF.
It was done by the creation of groves of "bays" which
permitted trees to grow near each other. The idea of the
"bay" originated when JNF foresters observed that the
landscapes along the roads were scarred by gulleys
formed by the action of rainwater This led to the
discovery that they could double the amount of rain
soaking into patches of land by building barriers across
the gulleys, thus capturing the flow of water into reser-
voirs. This water was used for growing forest trees and
eliminated the need for irrigating them in summer. The
first of these bays was prepared along the Beersheba-
Dimona road. Since then bays have been formed along
many of the roads in the Negev.

To adapt the old adage that, "A long journey starts
with a single step," an Israeli forester said, "A 75-year
old tree must start as a small seed." Today numerous
tree nurseries are scattered thoughout Israel, where
seedlings and saplings get a healthy start. After forestry
experts conduct research related to the soil,
water,insects and climate, a site is chosen, the soil ex-
amined, and the kind of trees to be planted determined.
The ground is cleared and the JNF Nursery at Eshtaol
in the Judean Hills, for example, is notified that 10,000
seedlings will be needed for planting the following May.

At the nursery, seedlings are nurtured in five-gallon
gasoline cans cut in half. Each can contains 10 treelets,

three to four inches high. Row upon row, the cans stand in parade formation, looking at a distance like a green corduroy bedspread.

A year later, the seedlings have doubled in height. They are hauled in their tin containers to the new forest area where holes will already have been dug. With a quick thrust of a handtool, each seedling is transferred from can to soil, where it begins its existence as a forest tree.

In this land of new forests, the ancient holiday Tu B'Shevat (the New Year of Trees) is a popular one. Children plant saplings and older people eat figs, almonds, raisins, dates, and bokser (the fruit of the carob tree) to recall the fruits mentioned in the Bible.

Another old custom, revived in modern Israel, is the planting of a cedar on the birth of a boy, which signifies strength and stature. On the birth of a girl, a cypress, standing for gracefulness and gentleness, is planted. The children tend the trees as they grow up, and when they marry, the branches are cut to support the wedding canopy.

Of all types of trees in Israel, it was the eucalyptus that proved to be a lifeline. It grew with greatest rapidity, with roots acting as virtual sponge to dry up the surplus water from the marshland. It became almost invaluable in the development of the country. Paradoxically, it is also the "camel" of trees, due to its ability to survive in the desert with little water.

The arrival of the eucalyptus into Israel has a unique history. In 1883, an American Christian missionary in Jerusalem, Horatio Spafford, received a packet of eucalyptus seeds from Australia and gave them to the headmaster of Mikvah Israel Agricultural School near Jaffa, which he planted at the school. Spafford wrote this comment in his diary: "May a mighty blessing come through these seeds to Palestine." His wish was granted as the eucalyptus became the mainstay of the country's forests. Thousands were later planted by the JNF to help drain the malaria-infested swamps and turn back the desert land.

The JNF workers originally experimented with 1700 different varieties of trees to meet the earth requirements of each type of soil. Three hundred are now thriving without irrigation. The trees that were found to be most successful in Israel's afforestation program are:

Jerusalem pine: best suited for hills and to implant roots on rocks.

Cypress: thrives both on hills and in plains.

Tamarisk: originally found in the Negev, is grown on saline soils and on sand. It proves useful as a windbreak.

Acacia: also takes root in the dry Negev soil and on coastal sand dunes. It is a fragrant, flowering tree that provides chemicals used in dyeing and tanning industries.

Carob: able to grow in the foothills. It is shady, beautiful, long-lived. Carob honey is popular throughout the Middle East and the fruit can be compressed into fodder for animals.

Pistachio: delicate and fragrant, yielding a valuable medicinal oil.

Olive: this silvery-green age-old tree is indispensible not only for its fruit and oil, but for its shade and beauty.

Nettle: not a bush, but a hardy tree native to Israel that is a member of the mulberry family.

Israel's successful application of its intensive experimental research in transforming barren soil into vast forests has attracted the world-wide attention of agronomists. As the result of her open door policy, she has shared her experience to help many countries. Experts in agronomy continue to come from Cyprus, Kenya, Germany, Switzerland, and from dry areas in the U.S. such as Nevada, to study Israel's operations in forestry, and to learn how her intensive soil preparation has led to the planting of forests where it would not have been possible. JNF experts were sent to a number of fledging African nations who profited from Israel's own early experience. Schools of afforestation also helped many Israeli settlers who were unfamiliar with forestry (the Jews from Yemen never saw a tree).

Trees served as a barrier of protecton for the new settlements in Israel. Every kibbutz and moshav was surrounded by forests, which acted as a camouflage. The trees also provided a shield against the winds and shifting sands.

Forests also helped raise the quality of life of the city dwellers in Israel, when the JNF opened them to the public for rest and recreation. Parks, camping grounds, playgrounds and picnic sites set up in the forests provide a haven for today's urban Israelis. Forests also combat air pollution by reducing wind velocities, causing dust to settle on the ground, and fumes to rise high in the air above the populace. Besides absorbing noise, the trees also serve to lower temperatures on hot days and counteract the dry desert winds by raising the moisture in the air.

It has been discovered that twelve types of trees in

Israel act as natural absorbers of air pollution caused by heavy industry, power stations, and motor vehicles. Some of the trees are kermes oak, terebrinth, letisk, phillyrea, olive, carob, and blue acacia. Research disclosed that despite the extent of pollution the trees were exposed to, the aborption of the poisons by the leaves permitted the trees to flourish and remain green. These trees, when planted close to homes near factories, serve as virtual vacuum cleaners for the surrounding air.

The use of the timber from forests as a by-product in the life and economy of the country is developing into an important asset. The need for large quantities of lumber is an increasing demand as raw material for fiber-board factories and for funiture making. Lumber is also used for small sawmills which manufacture poles, posts, fence stakes, crates, pegs, panels, and handles. For this purpose more than 145,000 cubic yards of wood were removed from Israel's forests in 1978.

The vast amounts of branches, twigs, and thin stems of trees are used for charcoal manufacture. Charcoal burners from villages situated near wooded areas obtain from the JNF a concession to remove these from the trees under close control and guidance by JNF foresters. Another product derived from trees is resin, extracted from the Aleppo Pine, which promises to be a valuable addition to Israel's economy.

As a symbol of immortality the JNF has planted forests in memory of great world figures. Forests bear the names of Israel's most distinguished leaders such as Theodor Herzl and Chaim Weizman, besides recording for all time the services rendered by great people outside of Israel, among them Lord Balfour, Winston Churchill,

John F. Kennedy, Harry S. Truman, Abraham Lincoln, Eleanor Roosevelt, Queen Elizabeth II, Louis S. Brandeis, and many other of the world's great personalities. Forests are also named after key individuals as well as worldwide communities which have made signal contributions to Israel. The Kennedy Forest, established by Jews and non-Jews alike in loving tribute to a president whose life was cut off in its prime, contains more than four million trees, and is part of the green belt surrounding Jerusalem. Two dominant forests are the mighty Martyr's Forest in the Judean Hills, an eternal monument to the six million murdered by the Nazis, and the Defender's Forest dedicated to the Jewish men and women who fell in World War II, and during the War of Independence.

The 200th Anniversary of the U.S.A. in 1976 was commemorated by the American Bicentennial National Park located on a restored barren stretch of land 13 miles outside of Jerusalem. The dedication ceremonies on July 4, 1976* took place on the hilltop overlooking the Judean Hills in the presence of Israeli President Efraim Katzir and United States Ambassador to Israel Malcolm Toon. The Stars and Stripes waved alongside the Blue and White flag in historic recognition of the partnership of the two democracies, the greatest alongside the smallest, banked by the forests of JNF-grown trees as worthy insignia of peace.

To perpetuate the memory of Senator Hubert Humphrey, the major highway leading to the American

---

*The day was also marked in history by the Israeli army's dramatic Entebbe rescue of the Jews who had been high-jacked on an Air France plane and flown to Uganda.

Bicentennial Park in Israel is being constructed as a joint Israel-American achievement and named the Hubert J. Humphrey Parkway. Not far from the Humphrey Forest which was planted near Jerusalem by the JNF in 1961, it symbolizes the late Senator's deep understanding of the binding relationship of the peoples of the United States and Israel. Apart from its function as a scenic driveway through the heart of the Bicentennial Park, the Humphrey Parkway serves as an important artery linking half a dozen of the villages in the Jerusalem hills with the Tell Aviv area. The dedication, on January 5, 1979 was attended by Prime Minister Begin along with United States Ambassador Lewis who said, "He loved Israel like he loved no other foreign nation. The Parkway is a great memorial to a great American."

X
ROADS AGAINST INROADS

Roads are the arteries of a nation, as essential to the life of a country as the flow of blood is to the life of the human body. The heart of Israel is Jerusalem; the lifeblood is pumped to and from it through its network of roads. It was in 1948, when Arab assaults had almost succeeded in cutting off Jerusalem, that Israel's Chief of Staff, General Yigael Yadin — a most unlikely military chief whose background was archaeology and scholarship — uncovered Biblical paths in the desert to turn the tide for the triumph in the War of Independence. The overnight building of these narrow paths into passable roads ("the Burma Road") made it possible for attack jeeps to encircle and ultimately defeat invading Arab forces which had already choked of the water supply of Jerusalem.

Throughout the newly-born state available roads became a vital factor in the victory of 1948, and provided Israel's armies with the means of essential mobility in the wars of 1956, 1967 and 1973. Where there were no roads as in the case of Kefar Etzion in 1948, settlements were overrun by the enemy and Jewish pioneers were murdered.

Since then, the JNF has undertaken a vast road-building program that ultimately was to bind the country with over 3,000 miles of roadways to skirt the border, pierce the deserts and cross the mountains. As a result of the many roads opened by the JNF, 100,000 acres of land which had previously been inaccessible were restored to Israel. Roads were instrumental in the establishment of Israeli villages in those regions.

In the early period of settlement in Palestine, hundreds of pioneer settlers would move in for the first stages of construction of a camp, to be followed almost immediately with road-building equipment brought in by the JNF to connect the new settlement with the outside world. Today, the pattern of new settlement has changed. Now a settlement *begins* with a road that leads to the proposed area, opening it up to development. It is then that the JNF's heavy earth-moving equipment is moved in to reclaim and develop the land. This is followed by bulldozers, which pave the road and make it possible for supplies, building materials to be brought in, and for the settlers to transfer their possessions to their new homes.

Each new site and every new village established in Israel has been opened by the JNF roads that lead to them. This has meant breaking into outlying regions previously cut off from the rest of the country. Areas like Yatir in the South could not formerly be reached at all. In 30 years of road blazing, the JNF has proved that by cutting new paths in the wasteland, roads give birth to new rural regions, new frontiers of settlement and forests which have since been linked by other JNF roads.

By making job opportunities accessible in remote areas, roads contribute increasingly to the economic development of the country. The JNF road from Sdom to Arad is an example. It runs through the stark, mountainous Judean desert, descending from the town on the plateau 640 meters above sea level to the lowest point on earth at the Dead Sea. Aside from opening up an entire part of the country, this road made it possible for the settlers of Arad to find their livelihood at the potash works at Sdom.

In agricultural settlements, indispensible roads make it possible for each cooperative to get its produce, while still fresh, to the local markets and the airport. They also provide the means of hauling raw materials to the farms and industrial enterprises for essential expansion.

The urban population of Israel is also benefited by avenues which open remote areas that otherwise would have remained closed and unknown to the public. The JNF cut roads through forests to create easily accessible recreation areas, camping grounds and picnic spots. Thanks also to the network of byways built by the JNF, thousands of city dwellers can commute daily between their homes and jobs, instead of having to wait until the weekend to return home, which was the case a few short years ago, before the roads and easy transportation existed.

Because the nation's economic well-being depends on it, speed is a major factor in JNF's road-building program. The new 25-mile desert highway from Jerusalem to the Dead Sea, which passes areas which were previously isolated from the national road network, was completed in record-breaking time. This road has opened up the new settlement of Tekoah in Judean Desert, and Herodion, the archaeological remains of Herod's summer palace. From there, the road runs southeast to Ein Gedi and Kibbutz Mitzpe Shalom, passing through breath-taking wadis and canyons near waterfalls which were previously inaccessible.

Roads that rim or lead to Israel's borders are essential for the nation's security. A security belt of border highways, some 248 miles long, touching on the frontiers of three Arab countries acts as a barrier for the protection of Israel's outlying areas.

These roads along the borders help protect Jews from terrorists who cross over from neighboring countries, usually at night, to unleash their havoc. In 1968, the JNF cut a "patrol road" along the Jordan Valley. Until that highway was built, 81 Israelis were killed. As the pathway opened to traffic, daily Army patrols were able to reduce the peril of assault until in 1972 there was only one border casualty in the area.

Another example of a highway serving defense needs is a 65-mile road which hugs the Lebanon border. This road protects the defenseless Huleh Valley farms at the foot of the Golan Heights and has proven its indispensibility in both the Six Day War and the Yom Kippur War when it served to help the Israeli Defense Forces to reach the battlefields quickly.

By opening desolate regions in Israel, JNF roads have been instrumental in the guarding of defense settlements along the borders. In these areas, the Adamit road on Lebanon's border, and roads in the Korazim and Almagor regions that once lay at the mercy of Syrian guns, helped protect those territories from Arab control and intimidation.

Several months before 1967, the JNF embarked on a major program of cutting roads near the armistice line to provide access to the settlements forming a protective barrier along the borders. These highways provided the means of quick access for the rapid shift of the defense forces from the Sinai to the Golan battlefields in the Six Day War and again in 1973.

The recapturing of Mount Hermon on the Golan Heights during the Yom Kippur War would not have been possible without the existence of the JNF road to that northernmost peak in Israel. This recent daring project created a highway which spirals up some 7,250 feet from the Druze village of Majdal Shams, "The Sun's Tower" on the Golan Heights up to Hermon's summit. When the sheer precipices were originally viewed by the overseer of the Hermon road cutting, he predicted it would be an "almost impossible job." It took three years for men and machines to reduce the mountain into a molehill, then a path, then a road base. Its 35 miles were perhaps the hardest and costliest ($46,000 per mile) to build. The boulders and the heights were also fraught with the danger of Fatah-men who sabotaged the work by mining the area, killing and injuring several workmen. Today the very presence of the road has driven the marauders away.

The roads built on the northern border at Metullah became not only essential for defense but served as a site for the "Good Fence,"* an Israeli operation of compassion. An escape hatch was cut through the barbed wire on the Lebanese side of the road to receive the Lebanese victims of the Civil War. Volunteer Israeli doctors and Lebanese nurses combined to tend the wounds and even deliver babies. The road would not have existed to serve the dual purpose of defense and mercy had it not been built by the JNF as part of its long-range program to connect remote and pivotal areas of the country. It is noteworthy that Lebanese workers are employed by the JNF.

---

* Israel set up clinics at the borders of Metullah and Har Dovev where doctors from the Hadassah Hospital treated more than 5,000 Lebanese (both Christian and Moslem) without payment during the Lebanese Civil War.

XI
SOCIAL BENEFITS TO THE STATE

There are priceless assets as by-products of JNF's work that have given stature, durability, and deep social benefits to the State. Newcomers in Israel arriving to face the rigors of barren soil and even bristling guns, were the beneficiaries of quick, responsive hospitable action from JNF. Employment opportunities had been prepared in advance to put them to work with all possible speed along with housing facilities which anticipated their personal needs. New citizens were blended into the new society as quickly and graciously as possible.

In 1949-1951, a period of mass immigration into Israel, thousands of newcomers were given jobs by JNF in a WPA-type operation of planting and caring for forests. The waves of new immigrants were employed, for example, in the Menasseh Hills, a plateau linking the Jezreel Valley with the coastal plain of Sharon, where a transit camp was set up by JNF to absorb hundreds of families, principally from Yemen, Iraq, and North Africa. They were all given work in a forest project.

When a recession period occurred before the Six Day War, the JNF was able to put 7,000 men to work daily. Along with its present vast program for Jewish workers, it is noteworthy that the JNF is the largest employer of Arabs in Israel.

The ownership of land purchased by the JNF carries with it an inherent element of social justice unique in the civilized world. Its contract contains the basic tenet, derived from the Bible, which provides in legal form that the land belongs inalienably to all the Jewish people. Since the JNF holds the land in trusteeship for the Jewish people everywhere, it is not possible for individuals to transfer or sell it in real estate transactions or otherwise. In the JNF contracts, which run for 49 years (and can be automatically renewed), holdings must be bequeathed to one single heir. Partition of the land surrounding a farm is also prohibited, as well as the joining together of several holdings into the estate of a single individual. This provision not only avoids farmsteads from being fragmented, but also prevents the emergence of large estates, a problem which is plaguing Arab states today.

The JNF contract for agricultural land contains an iron-clad protection from the use of the land for real estate sale and profiteering. The tenant is required to live permanently on the plot of land. His investment in it must be confined to his personal work. In this, he enjoys the freedom to decide on the manner of cultivation and the choice of crops, but he must utilize the land for agriculture only, and is obliged to apply adequate farming methods to refrain from any steps which might lead to soil erosion or any other deterioration of farming conditions.

It was the vision of the generation of JNF pioneers at the turn of the century which made possible the purchase and development of the land. Today's vision is turned to the future through reinvigoration from its youth. A wide-ranging educational program is an inherent part of the JNF operation geared to awaken this country's Jewish youth to the story of the rebirth of the homeland: to bring today's and future generations into a sense of joy in having a personal stake in the fruition of the land.

The JNF youth and Education Department serves as an information center and distributes materials such as stories and film, drama and educational games, wall posters and stamps to Jewish schools throughout the country. The publication of educational books, pamphlets and periodicals help to inform students and teachers about the dynamic history and current developments of the JNF in relation to the development of the State.

It is a year-round program, which traditionally culminates during the period of Tu B'shvat (the holiday of the planting of trees), closely identified with the JNF. As part of the holiday celebration, films are shown in schools which trace the development of trees through the careful nurturing of seeds, their unfolding into saplings, and growth into tall mature trees. Tree nurseries, some major JNF forests and scenes of the tree planting ceremonies on Tu B'Shevat in Israel are part of the dramatic showing to American youth.

To develop the student's identification with the people of Israel, the JNF organizes yearly tree-planting projects which bring Jewish youth closer to the soil with roots in the ongoing rebuilding of the nation. The special U.S. youth project for 1977 was the children's participation in the American Bicentennial Park. In 1978 the JNF conceived a far-reaching program, the Jewish Children's Forest. Over 100,000 youngsters throughout Europe and another 600,000 children in the United State received letters from children in Israel pledging to plant trees in their names in memory of the millions of youth who died in the Holocaust.

Children planting saplings for future forests, as part of the yearly tree planting projects which JNF organizes to bring Jewish youth closer to the soil with roots in the on-going rebuilding of the nation.

XII

THE JOY
OF
GIVING

The JNF became a spiritual tap-root that added a new dimension to the life of the Jewish people. It is a movement that captured the imagination and embodied the dreams of the Jewish masses — not the few but the many — linking their passionate desire for a sovereign State to a plan that became a reality, translating a fund into purchased land that anticipated and helped make possible, dunam by dunam, the sovereign state of Israel.

The nature and number of JNF programs offer Jews a variety of opportunities to forge an unbreakable link with Israel's development in a unique relationship between giver and the nation's progress. This opportunity is extended to Jews and non-Jews in various sections of the world through established representatives and offices.

Contributions to other Jewish organizations may disappear in the vast reservoir of funds and generally do not identify with specific Israeli programs, while the JNF offers numerous visible projects for Jews to enjoy a direct sense of participation and involvement with Israel's future. Among them are:

The Blue Box, an indestructible identity with the JNF to Jews everywhere, is an inseparable traditional symbol residing in millions of homes. The idea of the Blue Box was originated in 1902 in a letter to the Zionist publication *Die Welt* in Vienna by a clerk in a small town in Galicia who had taken a money box, written "National Fund" on it and placed it in his office. When he suggested that others might follow his example, the results led to the expansion of the habitual means of collecting money for the JNF. The first boxes were prepared and distributed in 1904 and became a familiar fixture in Jewish homes, shops, offices, synagogues and schoolrooms throughout the world. Even in Czarist Russia, where possession of the Blue Box was a peril, it was widely used. Boxes had to be smuggled into Russia by a JNF underground organization created for the purpose.

The shape and size of the box have undergone change over the years, but not the color that preceded the blue and white flag. Theodor Herzl was among the first to have a Blue Box in his home. The proceeds from the Blue Box are still a potent source of income to the JNF a century later.

The Golden Book in Jerusalem, where names are inscribed to honor those who have furthered the cause of Zionism, served as the basis for the first fund-raising activity for the JNF. Special adherents invited to inscribe their names for posterity. A year after the creation of the JNF in 1901, it was proposed that Herzl be the first to be inscribed in the Golden Book, but he stood aside in favor of Professor Hermann Schapira, who had inspired the concept of the Fund. Herzl took the second inscription. Since then, the Golden Book has become the "Hall of Fame" of the Jewish people, including many non-Jewish friends and supporters of Israel. Among the many distinguished American names that run like a golden thread through the book are President Harry S. Truman, Justice Louis D. Brandeis, Justice Felix Frankfurter, Louis Marshall, and Albert Einstein.

JNF Stamps: In a circular to the Russian Zionists in 1902, Menahem Ussishkin, one of the foremost pioneers of the JNF, stated: "To enable the redemption of Eretz Israel there has been inaugurated a system of stamp selling which will permit everyone to buy a stamp for a penny." That year the JNF issued its first stamp, a small blue and white seal with the work "Zion" inscribed within a Star of David surrounded by beams of light which became the stamp of the realm. From that date, over 2,000 separate individually designed stamps have been issued by the JNF, at first from Vienna and since 1921 from Jerusalem. Supporters throughout the years affixed JNF stamps to their letters along with those of the post office. (At first, the Turks suspected the Jews of producing their own stamps to defraud the Turkish post office.) The only time that JNF stamps were used for actual postage was in the very first days of the State of Israel when the government did not as yet have official postage stamps ready for use. Many Zionists considered it their duty to affix stamps to legal documents, telegrams, marriage licenses, and even to their door-posts, a democratic method of money collecting and identity with JNF.

The collection of JNF stamps forms a fascinating pic-torial review of Zionist history and the building of Israel. Their value has caused collectors to watch keenly for each new issue of the stamps. Many of the great tasks and exploits of the JNF over the years are vividly depicted. A stamp of special historic memory is the one commemorating the transition from Palestine to Israel. Stamps also portray personalities, public and religious institutions, sites and landscapes, settlements, major events, heroes and martyrs, Biblical quotations, and Jewish life throughout the world.

Planting of Trees: Since JNF's major work and identity are connected with acquisition and preparation of the Land in Israel, planting in the soil has become a virtual rite on the part of Jews the world over. As an invest-ment in immortality, it is unique in providing a means of identity with the soil so dear to the hearts of Jews. It is now a long-established way of honoring relatives, friends, and family. Contributions are made to the JNF for the planting of trees, a garden, a grove or a forest in its soil. A further step in creating links between forestry and the broad public is the "Plant the Tree with Your Own Hands" program where visitors, mainly from abroad (including many non-Jews) can themselves feel a part of the future upbuilding of the country by perform-ing the act of planting. Many non-Jews have par-ticipated in planting in the Land, in this way developing indigenous ties in support of the democratic society. Forests are planted in the name of outstanding in-dividuals or families whose names are designated with permanent markers on dedicatory walls near the the site of the planting.

As a happy means of dealing with the future of Israel, the Jewish Children's Forest, planted in honor of Israel's 30th year of independence is creating a bridge between Israeli children and Jewish youth throughout the world. Originated by the JNF chairman of the Board of Directors, Moshe Rivlin, an exchange of letters-between a child in Israel and a child from abroad pledge to plant three trees together. One is a tree in the name of the Israeli child, the second a tree in the name of the child abroad and a third tree in memory of one of the million children who died in the Holocaust and never lived to see the birth of a homeland for the Jews. The Jewish Children's Forest at Goren in the Western Galilee is part of the overall JNF plan in the broad development of the entire Galilee. A memorial grove will also be planted a Yad Vashem, the Holocaust Memorial in Jerusalem.

Nachlaot: The acquisiton and reclamation of a Nachlah, a tract of land of 10 dunams (two and a half acres) or more, offers a popular means of perpetual identification with the land of Israel, through the JNF. As an example, all JNF activity at the settlement of Hatzeva at the northern end of the Arava is being funded by such contributions from the American Jewish community. A Nachlah is valued at $10,000 or more.

Sefer Bar (or Bat) Mitzvah: A special register in Jerusalem in which children may be inscribed for special occasions such as their birth, birthday, recovery from illness, or first school day is the Sefer Hayeled.

At the time of their thirteenth birthday, or religious "coming of age", their names may be included in the

Sefer Bar or Bat Mitzvah. This book chronicals the risinggeneration of Jews upon whom will depend the future of the Jewish people, its traditions, and culture. The inscription of the names in the Sefer Bar or Bat Mitzvah which is preserved in the office of the Keren Kayemeth in Jerusalem, creates a vital link between the Bar and Bat Mitzvah and the land of Israel.

Planned Giving: The Foundation for the Jewish National Fund is an answer for those who wish to spread their joy of giving over the years and prefer to contribute through wills, bequests, insurance and annuities. To an increasing extent, adherents of the JNF are using the form of "Living Legacies" which in effect provides a double joy and satisfaction in giving. It ensures a regular income for their own later years, and at the same time helps strengthen the financial base of the Fund. A capital sum made over to the JNF provides a guaranteed life annuity.

A gift to the JNF Foundation can link the donor's name eternally to the land of Israel through any one of a number of JNF projects. Appropriate markers and certificates in the donor's name, or in the names of others that may be designated, will be prepared in recognition of his farsighted generosity. There are many other vital projects through which to become a sponsor with a legacy to Israel which will provide one a sense of being part of a legend forever.

The acceptance of the JNF's versatile avenues for spreading contributions over the years is indicated by the expansion of the Foundation's fund each year since 1948. Present, as well as future guaranteed income via the Foundation for the JNF now totals over $34,000,000 and is still growing.

XIII
DESTINATION

The prospects and preparation for Israel's new era of peace have roots in these indispensable historic achievements of the Jewish National Fund:

JNF owns 675,000 acres, or 15% of the land. Next to the State it is the largest landowner in Israel.

One out of every three inhabitants of Israel lives on JNF land.

160,000 acres of land that would have remained barren have been reclaimed by the JNF since 1901.

2,200 miles of roads have been built by the JNF.

170,000 acres of land have been planted for trees and forests.

850 settlements have been built on sites prepared by the JNF.

On the very day of the signing of the Peace treaty with Egypt — March 26, 1979 — the Board of Directors of the Keren Kayemeth LeIsrael (JNF) in Israel, adopted an unprecedented budget of $100,000,000 a year, a stunning figure exceeding three times anything contemplated before by the worldwide organization.

At the National Assembly of the Jewish National Fund of America, held in New York City on March 19, 1979, Moshe Rivlin, Chairman of the Keren Kayemeth LeIsrael called upon American Jewry to do its share in the new era of the nation. He said:

"The JNF is facing challenges we did not know before. For me it is not the price of peace, but the song of peace. That song must be a song that we will all sing together. It must be a song that Jews everywhere will be proud to become partners in that challenge of peace. It is a song that I wish and pray — years from now, when you or your children or your grandchildren, go through the Negev and the Galil — will be able to say, "I helped to achieve this."

The hub of the JNF's vast new operation extends into the wide expanses of the Negev and in the mountains of the Galilee. The organization has geared its resources first for the mammoth undertakings called for in the peace treaty; the removal of 20 settlements within three years from the Sinai to new localities in the Negev. Also, as part of a long-range project in the Negev, a half dozen pilot settlements are initiating a chain of 100 to 150 settlements that will run in a line adjacent to Yamit on the Sea, and to Eilat on the west. Another line of some 30 settlements will be built from the Dead Sea to Eilat on the east. In addition, there is continuing JNF work in expansion of road building, drainage and water storage throughout the country.

In the Arava, located in the eastern stretches of the Negev, where a dead landscape has become alive with thirteen JNF settlements, 20 more villages are being-planned. Also underway are new JNF projects which include the construction of high earth dams to divert the occasional disastrous flood waters which pour down from Mount Edom and other high mountains in Jordan. To fill the vacuum of dry sand, the JNF is transporting fertile soil into the settlements from vast distances to create new fields on arid sites in the Arava where agricultural growth had been unthinkable.

The critical area is the Galilee, where two thirds of the region is inhabited by non-Jews. The Arab inhabitants who dominate the region are ready to assault the Israelis. This could mean an insurrection from within, with dire consequences to the State. Israel is preparing to help meet this challenge with an immense JNF project which comprises the planning and building of 79 new settlements. In their fulfillment the very security of Israel is at stake.

Villages that have long been plagued by poverty in the Galilee are to be relieved and enhanced by the creation of industrial cooperatives. Plans call for settling 15,000 new immigrants together with 32,000 Israelis from the coastal plains and from central Israel in some 126,000 acres. A total of 20 to 35 new communities are to be established, some starting as Nahal (Army Pioneer Settlers Corps) settlements. This will mean the creation of

46,000 new jobs in agriculture and the service industries as well as the doubling of the number of farming units in the region. In the next five years, more than 1,700 new units in 34 settlements are scheduled to be added in sites in the Galilee.

The showcase of current JNF land development activity in the Galilee is the Segev bloc, covering an area of some 6,000 acres, most of which was unsuitable for cultivation and difficult to irrigate. A radically new settlement concept combines the moshav with an industrial village. Eight settlements of this type are planned for Segev, including an industrial zone, education, and service centers. The first of the new villages, Ya'ad, has been completed, and its settlers are already moving into their new homes.

Ya'ad is a computer town, in which the residents work in all the fields connected with planning and design by computer. The JNF was responsible for all the land preparation for Ya'ad, including clearing the ground for housing, for the large hothouses which grow plants for commercial sale, for the community center, and most importantly, for the computer complex.

A Galilee industrial plan consists of a belt of villages, stretching from Ma'alot in the Upper Galilee to Carmiel farther south. The first stage of this plan is the industrial zone of Tefen, just outside of Ma'alot, which will incorporate five major industries. Of these, a battery-and-appliance plant is already in production, a rubber processing plant is in the final stages of construction, and a shoe factory is now being established. Surrounding Tefen, for which the land development was sponsored by Hadassah, a ring of six residential communities is envisaged, somewhat along the lines of the Segev bloc.

The JNF's expanding program for the State now in progress is based upon a Five Year Plan announced by Moshe Rivlin in mid-1977. Under the plan the JNF is providing a new dimension to the critical areas now dormant by transforming them into fertile regions, adding significantly to the productive capacity of the nation.

FIVE YEAR PROGRAM 1977/8 to 1982/3

Land reclamation	37,5000 acres
Farming	15,000 Farming units
Rural housing	7,500 Rural housing units
Drainage	12,500 acres
Roads	1,240 miles
New forest planting	37,500 acres
Care of existing forests	168,750 acres
Parks and recreation grounds	1,000 recreation units

An expectation of a population growth of five million for Israel be 1990 is at the base of the plan. The absorption of the added population is anticipated by the JNF through its vast building program of new communities.

PRIORITIES FOR THE EIGHTIES

The JNF is introducing a major program of priorities in the 1980's to fortify the nation's position. One involves the project earmarking 125,000 acres of land for agricultural purposes. In addition, JNF will develop land resources in the crucial Galilee, blast roads and form networks in the Negev and Judean Deserts.

High priority will be given in an area known as the Negev Peace Salient. The Negev will not be left as a military base once the Israeli Forces withdraw from Sinai. Alongside the airfields, camps, training grounds, a civilian population is planned for settlement based on agriculture and light industry. Here in the northwest corner of the Negev, the JNF has already leveled 6,400 acres of sand dunes for setting up a bloc of agricultural settlements. By January, 1982, with Israel's withdrawal from Sinai, preparation of the remaining settlement sites will have been completed. Six moshavim as well as two kibbutzim have already agreed to move from northern Sinai to the new "Peace Salient." Building began early in 1980 and throughout the year JNF bulldozers continued levelling the sand dunes for further construction. When completed, 500 million cubic meters of earth will have been moved. Expectations are high that this development of the Negev will make it the "granary" of Israel.

In the Galilee, where there are 160,000 acres of State-owned land, half under direct or indirect Arab control, the most urgent program has been undertaken. Thirty-one new settlements had been established in 1980 aimed at deterring the rapid progress of Arabs from taking control of vast sections of the area. As any square meter of land not occupied by Jews would be in Arab hands, speed has been the watchword of JNF planners. Small settlements—"mitzpim" (lookout posts housing 15 to 25 families) and "mitzporim" (smaller posts with five to seven families)—were quickly established throughout the Galilee in strategic ridgeline locations on mountain tops.

These preliminary settlements, with the settlers living in small prefabricated houses under simple means, will later be transformed into regular permanent villages, designed to gain control of over 40,000 acres of land. Fourteen more "mitzpim" are planned for the Galilee in the next two years.

Moshe Rivlin, Chairman of the JNF directorate, stressed the work's importance: "Of the 280,000 acres in the Galilee hills, 82,500 are controlled by Arab residents and only 32,500 by Jews. Furthermore, Arabs have been making greater incursions into the 160,000 acres of public land, which the mini-settlements are designed to curb. Today the 'mitzpim' give us control of over 25,000 to 30,000 acres."

Rivlin also noted that the JNF is involved in a massive land improvement plan in the Eshkol Region bordering the Gaza Strip. For each of the 20 settlements being prepared, more than a million cubic meters of sand has to be levelled. In addition, ground that had never been farmed has to be made suitable for agriculture. Here and elsewhere in the country, new techniques are permitting the transformation of marginal land into profitable agricultural land. In this way, hundreds of thousands of acres can now be brought to life.

In the next few years, the JNF will also be creating the foundation for new settlements in the Arava and the Sodom area besides the northern Negev. By the year 2000 the JNF expects to add 125,000 acres of forests to the quarter million acres that presently exist.

Throughout its 80-year history, the JNF has made its expertise available to other developing nations, especially in Africa and Asia. And it is entirely possible that the next nation to benefit from JNF know-how is Egypt. It is the dream of President Sadat that the vast deserts of his own land can be redeemed in the same manner that the soil of Israel was restored by the Jewish National Fund.

One of Moshe Rivlin's signal announcements was JNF's plan of a "Peace Park" which will constitute the new border with Egypt following the completion of the Israeli withdrawal from Sinai."I have a dream," he concluded,"to see the park extended by the Egyptians on their side of the border."

XIV
JNF
AND THE
AMERICAN EXPERIENCE

One cannot read the dramatic epic of Israelis pushing the deserts back to establish frontiers for an independent democratic state without sensing its affinity with the American experience. The early history of America is in large measure the story of pioneering adventure in penetration and cultivation of vast neglected areas. While the Americans' early struggle was against the wilderness, the Israelis were obliged to conquer the desert. It is an ironic coincidence of history that the political struggle of the United States and Israel in their formative stages was against the same foreign power, Great Britain.

Nor was it the hostile neighbor, the feudal Arab lord who was the total enemy that the Israelis faced, but the resistance of the desolate, encrusted land from centuries of waste and neglect. The Arabs fought back not only with guns but against the very cultivation of the land that separates them.

Israel is a modern microcosm of the freedom story. Will Americans ever forget the drama of their "minutemen," whose instant answer to the call to meet the assault of a foreign mercenary army saved the Colonists? Future generations of Israelis will likewise remember with legendary pride how their own stalwart people were called without notice to bear arms in four wars to secure their infant state.

Can a deeper kinship exist between two peoples than the knowledge that they, the largest and smallest democracies, sprang from an identical belief in the democratic ideal? This kinship has been solidified by the many visits and inspections by Americans to share with Israelis their techniques and success in creating forests out of wasteland. Israel is indeed the living proof that democracy is as strong as its weakest link. Small in size, but greatly enlarged by the fount of strength which it draws from the deep well of its heritage, its structure is built from the ground up, with grassroots made possible and reinforced by the indispensable arm of the Jewish National Fund.

Not unlike the American experience, its imperishable treasure was found in the turning of the soil from its years of weariness and slumber from breathing into it life and awakening.

Zionism was a revolution against history, the JNF was a rebellion against geography. The JNF refused to take geography for granted. Deserts and mountains, long neglected and abandoned, had no value in themselves until they were lovingly and scientifically treated. What others accepted, the JNF challenged, taking upon itself the task of altering the geography of the country. Jews the world over became partners through the JNF in permitting the earth to perform a task originally assigned to it.

I.H.

טקס הקדשה
דרך הוברט ה'המפרי
פארק 200 שנות ארצות הברית

DEDICATION CEREMONY
HUBERT H HUMPHREY PARKWAY

State Senator Hubert H. Humphrey III (Minn.) with JNF Executive Vice President Dr. Samuel I. Cohen at the dedication ceremony of the Hubert H. Humphrey Parkway in the American Bicentennial Park outside Jerusalem, January, 1979.

POSTSCRIPT

It is from Jerusalem that I write. The time, Spring 1979. From the heart of this ancient nation, I return to the scene that gave this book its birth.

It was rediscovery. Then revelation. And awakening.

From what better locale could an appraisal of the 78 years of achievement of the JNF be made than on the scene in the cultivated narrow geography now called Israel? It was as though the prophets handed the script to the JNF pioneers to perform the task at this newly appointed time in history to do battle not against neighbors who had heard only the wind of desolation in the wilderness, but against the barrenness of the land to which it would now give new life and meaning as part of a timeless inheritance.

At my feet lay the soil which I had first seen as crusty waste, now spread out before me into a veritable green belt. The hand of the spade had been firm in the turning of the earth, yielding its untold secret in fruits and

flowers. Looking up from my musings, flashes of tur-
bulence come back from my early encounters with the
British imperialists in this capitol like distant thunder
of a storm that has struck and moved on. Suddenly, out
of the sun's haze, a phantom figure appears: it is Joseph
Weitz — that dynamo of passionate devotion to the earth,
who had invited me in 1945 on my return from Turkey to
join with him on a day's expedition to scratch the skeletal
soil and to experience the sure response to his gentle
unerring fingers.

I descend from Jerusalem on the road bordering the
ancient gray walls of the old city down the hairpin turns
of the Judean Hills into the Jordan Valley through sleepy
Jericho past endless miles of sand called the West Bank
leading to the steep inclines toward the Dead Sea. The
curving hills scallop the edges of the cloudless sky. I climb
to the shores of Galilee and circle Lake Tiberius.

Before me stands a forest of trees, living proof of the
"marriage" of JNF with the earth. The wilderness is
now verdant life. Giant cypress and eucalyptus sway
gently in the wind, harbingers of Israel's upward reach
for universal harmony.

The narrowing desert stretches out into roads lined
like tents with tall cypresses and Jerusalem pines that
blend into the sky, nurtured by JNF - the earth's hosts.
Now an undulating plateau leads up to Mount Hermon,
soaring thousands of feet above, sloping down its steep
elevation still white with snow. From here I breathe the
unending ether and see the face of mankind.

As I scan the landscape, my eye is interrupted by a single grey-green olive tree, its gnarled branches unbroken by the decades that eroded the trunk's surface, but not the core. Thick with maturing fruit, its twisted arms still reached upward.

Did I see in this veritable patriarch of nature an extended <u>olive branch</u>, that proud timeless symbol of peace, now proferred by the unwavering hand of the Israelis to her Arab neighbors? Humbled, I was in the presence of the awakening.

Olive tree, patriarch of Israel's landscape, with its extended "olive branch," timeless symbol of peace, proferred by the unwavering hand of the Israelis to her Arab neighbors.

THE ROLE OF THE
JEWISH NATIONAL FUND
IN THE CONTEXT OF A
MIDDLE EAST PEACE AGREEMENT
by Dr. Samuel I. Cohen
Executive Vice-President

The Israel-Egypt peace treaty which ushered in a new, era for the entire Middle East, represents an unprecedented challenge to the Jewish National Fund in the areas of planning, development, road blazing, and land reclamation. Once again, the JNF is being charged with an historic responsibility for a new "awakening" of the land.

Since its inception nearly eighty years ago, the JNF has served with fidelity as the sole body responsible for the care and development of the land of Israel. In 1947, when the United Nations proposed the creation of a Jewish State from a portion of the British mandate in Palestine, the outline of that state was largely determined by lands held in trust for the Jewish people throughout the world by the Jewish National Fund.

Throughout its proud history, JNF has successfully responded to every demand imposed upon it by the needs of the reborn State. Whenever an urgent need for a settlement arose, JNF was there first, to solve the myriad of problems created by the charting of new territories. In fulfillment of its role in the practical application of the ideological values of Zionism, the JNF literally built the country acre by acre, first by purchasing dunam after dunam of land, and afterwards, by developing each dunam through ongoing programs of afforestation and soil reclamation.

Since the creation of the State, the JNF has been responsible for the access roads leading to each new site and every new village created in Israel. In border areas, these roads took on the added significance of a network essential to national security. For the road is the lifeline of each agricultural settlement, enabling its produce to get to the local markets and to the airport for export while it is still fresh. And roads are necessary for hauling raw materials to farms and industrial centers so they may continue to expand and develop. During the past 30 years, the JNF has blazed more than 3,500 kilometers of roads across deserts, along the borders, over mountains, and through the most forbidding terrain.

Another primary function of the JNF has been in the area of afforestation. To bring the forests closer to man and to bring man closer to his natural environment...this is the concept upon which the JNF's afforestation plan is based. For the JNF, afforestation began as a symbol of existence. "We plant, therefore we are here," was drawn from the biblical commandment to plant trees of all kinds upon coming to the land of Israel. In the early days of the State, planting trees was more than symbolic. It was a way to facilitate resettlement of the population along borders in new and far-away settlements by providing the new settlers with a livlihood.

Since Israel's statehood, the JNF has increased its afforested area by more than half a million dunams. While forests cannot offer a total solution to the problems of pollution, they can made a marked contribution toward its alleviation. Thus, JNF has planted trees in urban areas to act as buffer zones, separating industrial from residential areas. It has "installed" trees around polluting sources, such as factories or power stations, to serve as natural barriers that prevent the dissemination of pollutant particles; and it has planted forests to abate noise and to cool temperatures of surrounding regions.

When the State of Israel came into being, emphasis shifted from land purchase to land reclamation. The JNF concentrated its efforts upon vast land reclamation projects to open the way for the resettlement of hundreds of thousands of immigrants. In the early years of statehood, it was the the JNF's drainage work which transformed many of Israel's swampy regions into fertile farmland or industrial centers. This included the building of canals, the laying of underground pipes, and the opening of outlets for stagnant waters in the valleys. These were experimental pilot projects which set the precedent for the far-reaching agricultural drainage work which followed, changing thousands of dunams of waterlogged, oversaturated sub-soil into the black, rich soil which has made Israel self-sustaining agriculturally. In the Galilee, the JNF cut deep canals away from the fields, directing the waters to a nearby course. In extremely saline areas, such as the Arava and lower Jordan Valley which lack natural drainage outlets, the JNF flooded future fields to rinse the soil and make it cultivable. As a result, the Arava and Jordan Valley have become centers of highest quality export fruit and vegetables. The problem that remains is the scarcity of water in the extensive expanses of desert in Israel, like the Negev. To overcome this, the JNF has set up reserviors all over the country to collect rain water for maximum conservation of all available water supplies.

Today, in the context of the peace accord, all of these programs take on an added dimension of meaning. For now, the JNF has been given a mission of unprecedented scope and urgency...to help relocate the settlers from the Sinai by preparing the sites for 20 new settlements in the Negev, and to plan for new centers of Jewish life in the Galilee...in short, to build a new land of plenty, and create a lasting legacy of peace.

As a result of the terms of the peace agreement, the Negev, which in ancient times was densely populated, again assumes the highest degree of national importance. It must again be made a habitable center throbbing with life. New areas capable of absorbing all the settlements that will have to be transferred must be developed. Planning activities are currently underway in the sand dunes southeast of the existing settlements, in a region appropriately named the Peace Salient, where prepatory work for the establishment of 20 settlements has already begun. Likewise, in the Arava and Sidom Desert Valley, the JNF is in the forefront of developing area surveys, planning roads and land reclamation, and paving the way for the agencies who will follow to construct the new settlements.

Similarly, JNF faces new and urgent challenges in settling and developing the Galilee. There, for political, economic, security, and demographic reasons, the area of 275,000 acres must be developed. A total of 15,000 new immigrants must be resettled, together with 32,000 Israelis from the coastal plains and from central Israel. Some 46,000 new jobs, ranging from agriculture to the service industries, must be created, and from 20-25 new communities must be established. In this vital area JNF's role is to prepare hundreds of farm/housing units, replete with necessary infrastructure, both in existing moshavim and villages and in new settlements. As part of this task, JNF already has completed preparing more than 2,400 acres for new orchards and irrigation.

In addition to these priority projects, the JNF will also implement a Five-Year Plan to prepare 150,000 dunams of wastelands for intensive farming and lay foundations for the construction of 15,000 new production units and 7,500 homes for rural settlers. In all, the Plan envisions the preparation of infrastructure for 185 villages by the year 1990, resulting in the more even distribution of the country's population and the enlargement of the urban and rural centers of Galilee, the Negev, and other out-lying regions. This means land reclamation in its most complicated and extensive forms.

It means moving tons upon tons of rocks in the Galilee to reach the hidden soil.

It means anchoring sand dunes and enriching the desert soil of the Negev.

It means creating new land in the Arava by "transplanting" fertile soil from other regions.

It means building sophisticated infrastructure to ready the land for the modern installations needed for the growth of new settlements — giant hothouses, automated poultry runs, factories, stables and barns, tourist facilities, tropical fruit gardens, extensive flower beds, etc.

And in the area of afforestion, new policies have been initiated that will open the forests to the people and introduce new factors in creating Israel's ecological balance.

Now, in a modern Israel rapidly approaching the threshold of the 21st century, the JNF is preparing plans and blueprints to meet the ecological and environmental demands of a growing nation so that it may take its rightful place in a highly complex, industrialized age. By 1990, Israel's population is expected to reach more than 5,000,000 — nearly double its present size. Only the quantity of land will remain constant. Thus, preserving Israel's quality of life demands that sufficient area be left as open spaces. Under JNF's aegis, cities will be intersected with park-like woods and surrounded by green belts of trees, while highways running through arid plains of yellow dust and sand will be skirted by stately rows of eucalyptus providing both shade and protection from the inroads of erosion and flash floods. Trees will be planted in urban areas, separating the industrial from the residential areas. JNF will continue to develop these forests as natural preserves against the adverse affects of modern civilization upon man, so that the people of Israel will have a "green escape" from the ever-more crowded and confined word of asphalt and concrete.

Caring and developing the land of Israel...assuring its physical welfare...protecting it from misuse, encroachments, and hostile elements. For decades, JNF has fought an epic ecological battle against pollution and the ravages of man and nature in a concerted effort to make the deserts bloom. These have been the historic responsibilities of the Jewish National Fund since its formation. Today, in the first year of peace that Israel has known, they are being fulfilled with undiminished vigor.

BIBLIOGRAPHY

1. Dr. Alex Bein, *The Return to the Soil, A History of Jewish Settlement in Israel,* Youth & Hechalutz Dept. of the Zionist Organization, Jerusalem, 1952.

2. Hanoch Beniyaha (compiler), *And the Land Responded,* Keren Kayemeth LeIsrael, Jerusalem, 1978.

3. Adolph Boehm and Adolph Pollak, *Jewish National Fund,* Keren Kayemeth LeIsrael, Jerusalem, 1939.

4. A. Granott, *Agrarian Reform and the Record of Israel,* Eyre & Spottiswood, London, 1956.

5. A. Granott, *The Land System in Palestine,* Eyre & Spottiswoode, London, 1952.

6. Moshe Levin, *The Story of the Jewish National Fund,* Jewish National Fund, Jerusalem, 1954.

7. Isaac Mann and Baruch Sarel (editors), *Creating Soil,* Keren Kayemeth LeIsrael, Jerusalem, 1956.

8. Harry Milt, *Israel's Fight for Life,* American Zionist Federation, New York, 1971.

9. Efraim Orni, *Afforestation in Israel,* Keren Kayemeth LeIsrael, Jerusalem, 1969.

10. Efraim Orni, *Agrarian Reform and Social Progress in Israel,* Keren Kayemeth LeIsrael, Jerusalem, 1972.

11. Efraim Orni, *Forms of Settlement,* Keren Kayemeth LeIsrael, Jerusalem, 1976

12. Joseph Weitz, *Forests and Afforestation in Israel,* Massada Press, Jerusalem, 1974.

APPENDIX

PRESIDENTS OF THE J.N.F.

Rabbi William Berkowitz	1977-
Meyer Pesin	1976-1977
Dr. Maurice S. Sage	1975-1976
Meyer Pesin	1971-1975
Herman L. Weissman	1966-1971
Max Bressler	1964-1966
Albert Schiff	1960-1964
Dr. H. J. Levine	1950-1960
Morris Rothenberg	1943-1950
Israel Goldstein	1933-1943
Nelson Ruttenberg	1931-1933
Emanuel Neumann	1928-1931
Joseph Barondess	1928-
Dr. Joseph Krimsky	1926-1928
Bernard A. Rosenblatt	1924-1926
Senior Abel	1912-1924
David H. Lieberman	1910-1912

EXECUTIVE VICE PRESIDENTS OF THE J.N.F.

Dr. Samuel I. Cohen	1977-
Abram Salomon	1971-1976
Dr. Milton Aron	1965-1971
Rabbi Joseph Sternstein	1962-1964
Mendel Fisher	1935-1962

CONSTITUENT J.N.F. ORGANIZATIONS IN THE U.S.

Zionist Organization of America
Hadassah
Hashomer Hatzair
Labor Zionist Alliance
Pioneer Women
Religious Zionist of America
American Mizrachi Women
Bnai Zion
Herut U.S.A.
United Zionists-Revisionists of America
American Jewish League for Israel

CHAIRMEN OF THE BOARD OF DIRECTORS OF THE KEREN KAYEMETH L'ISRAEL

Moshe Rivlin	1977-
Jacob Tsur	1960-1977
Dr. A. Granott	1945-1960
Dr. A. Granott, Rabbi M. Bar-Ilan and Berl Katznelson	1941-1944
Menahem M. Ussishkin	1922-1941

OBSERVERS

B'nai B'rith
North-American Jewish Youth Council
Union of American Hebrew Congregations
United Synagogue of America

JNF WORLD-WIDE OFFICES

AMERICA
United States of America
Canada
LATIN AMERICA &
SOUTH AMERICA
Argentina
Bolivia
Brasil
Chile
Colombia
Costa Rica
Curacao - N.A.
Rep. Dominicana
Ecuador
El Salvador
Guatemala
Honduras
Mexico
Nicaragua
Panama
Paraguay
Peru
Uruguay
Venezuela

EUROPE
Austria
Belgium

Denmark
Finland
France
Germany
Great Britain and Ireland
Greece
Holland
Italy
Luxembourg
Norway
Sweden
Switzerland
Spain
ASIA
Iran
AFRICA
South Africa
Rhodesia
AUSTRALIA
NEW ZEALAND

JEWISH NATIONAL FUND (KEREN KAYEMETH LEISRAEL), INC.
OFFICERS AND ADMINISTRATIVE COMMITTEE
1979-1981

President
RABBI WILLIAM BERKOWITZ

Honorary Presidents

DR. ISRAEL GOLDSTEIN   DR. EMANUEL NEUMANN
MEYER PESIN   HERMAN L. WEISMAN

Vice Presidents

MRS. D. LEONARD COHEN   I. K. GOLDSTEIN
MOSHE KAGAN   ROBERT B. LEVINE
MRS. ELI RESNIKOFF

Treasurer
MORRIS LIFSCHITZ

Associate Treasurers

MRS. HENRY GOLDMAN   JACK LEFKOWITZ

Secretary
MRS. ZELDA LEMBERGER

Honorary Secretary
LEON RUBINSTEIN

*Adminstrative Committee

M. JOSEPH BAER   MRS. RUTH POPKIN
HYMAN ARBESFELD   HERMAN Z. QUITTMAN
LEWIS CAPLAN   MRS. HELENA SALOMON
ISIDORE GOLDZIMER   HENRY SHOR
MRS. ISIDORE GOLDZIMER   MRS. ANNA TULIN
MENACHEM JACOBI   MRS. HARRY WEISENFELD
MAX LEWKO   MRS. ELSIE WATTENBERG

Ex-Officio:

DR. SAMUEL I. COHEN   DR. ARON WEINBERGER

*In addition to the above listed Officers

Honorary Chairpersons

RABBI LOUIS BERNSTEIN
MRS. SHIRLEY BILLET
PINCHAS CRUSO
MRS. MOSES P. EPSTEIN
RABBI ROLAND B. GITTELSOHN
MRS. CHARLOTTE JACOBSON
MRS. NORMAN LEEMON
RABBI IRVING LEHRMAN
JUDGE SEYMOUR R. LEVINE
RABBI ISRAEL MILLER
MRS. LAURA MOVCHINE

IVAN J. NOVICK
PROF. ALLEN POLLACK
PAUL SAFRO
MRS. RAYMOND SILBERSTEIN
ERYK SPEKTOR
ABRAHAM SPIEGEL
JACK J. SPITZER
DR. JOSEPH P. STERNSTEIN
BEN SWIG
MRS. NATHAN TANNENBAUM
JACK D. WEILER

Honorary Vice-Chairpersons

THE HON. ROBERT ABRAMS
RABBI MAYER ABRAMOWITZ
PROF. HOWARD L. ADELSON
JUDGE DAVID AISENSON
MAURICE ARONOWITZ
BENJAMIN N. BERGER
DAVID S. BERN
HAROLD BERNSTEIN
DAVID M. BLUMBERG
LOUIS BOGOPULSKY
MRS. AARON BURACK
AVRUM M. CHUDNOW
SAMUEL COHEN
MRS. MOSES DYCKMAN
JACOB FELDMAN
MRS. BLANCHE FINE
MRS. NATHAN B. FISCHER
GEORGE GELLER
MORRIS GILONI
HENRY GOLDMAN
HYMEN GOLDMAN
JACOB GOODMAN
ABRAHAM GRUNHUT
BERNARD HARKAVY
ALEXANDER HASSAN
MRS. ALEXANDER HASSAN
GEORGE L. HECKER
IRA HIRSCHMANN
LAWRENCE G. HOROWITZ
BURTON M. JOSEPH
MRS. SIEGFRIED KRAMARSKY
MRS. CLARA LEFF
MRS. AARON LEIFER

MRS. DOROTHY S. LEVINE
RABBI ISRAEL H. LEVINTHAL
ELEAZAR LIPSKY
RABBI IRVING MILLER
JUDGE ABRAHAM J. MULTER
RABBI JACOB OTT
ERNEST NATHAN
BENJAMIN NIGROSH
RAYMOND M. PATT
MRS. ESTHER PEVSNER
MRS. AL PINCUS
JAMES B. RADETSKY
BERNARD ROSENBERG
SENATOR WILLIAM ROSENBLATT
DR. MIRIAM FREUND ROSENTHAL
RABBI HERSCHEL SCHACTER
RABBI ALEXANDER M. SCHINDLER
RABBI ARTHUR SCHNEIER
MRS. LOUIS J. SCHREIBER
DR. JUDAH J. SHAPIRO
JUDGE BURTON R. SHIFAM
MRS. SYLVAN M. SHANE
MERVIN SHPRITZ
PHILIP SLOMOVITZ
MRS. CHARLOTTE STEIN
CHARLES L. TABAS
DANIEL M. TABAS
MRS. LOUIS WALD
MRS. TOBY WILLIG
HARRY L. WOLL
BERT L. WOLSTEIN
PAUL ZUCKERMAN

Associates

ROBERT ABRAMS
ZOLLIE BARATZ
JACK BECKER
EDWARD W. BERGER
MORRIS J. BRANDWINE
JUDGE MEYER M. CARDIN
JEFFREY N. COHEN
DR. ALAN EBERSTEIN
SHOOLEM ETTINGER
JAY L. FIALKOW
MRS. MIRIAM FINKELSTEIN
RABBI EZRA GELLMAN
JACK GEDDY GLODBERG
MAX GOLDFIELD
HENRY GOLDMAN
MRS. REGINA GORDON
JUDGE BARRY GRANT
LARRY HAITH
EDWIN F. HARRIS
MARTIN HOFFMAN
DAVID B. HOLTZMAN
DR. PAUL HURWITZ
MRS. KEEVA KEKST
BENNET KLEINMAN
MRS. BENNET KLEINMAN
DR. MARTIN KRASNY

MRS. LEONARD KRAVITZ
DR. HAROLD KUSHNER
MILTON LEVENFELD
ARTHUR J. LEVINE
STANLEY LOUIS
IRVING LINDEN
CYRIL MAGNIN
DR. MAYER MEHLER
ABE NUTKIS
MRS. MEYER PESIN
LOUIS PISER
RABBI ALBERT PLOTKIN
GARY RABINER
ALLECK A. RESNICK
ROBERT ROBIN
DR. ADOLF C. ROBISON
MRS. ANNE ROBISON
HERBERT ROSENBERG
ROBERT B. ROTTMAN
JULIUS SCHATZ
RABBI NISON SHULMAN
MRS. FRANK SILVERMAN
JULIUS SOMMER
JACOB STEIN
DR. ISRAEL WIENER
ARTHUR ZIMMERMAN

Directors-At-Large

STANFORD BENSON
RABBI GILBERT EPSTEIN
GILBERT GERTNER
MEYER HALPERIN

JACK MITTLEMAN
JOSEPH SALOMON
DR. ALVIN SCHIFF
DR. GILBERT WILDSTEIN

NORMAN P. ZARWIN

Observers

B'NAI B'RITH   M. NATHAN CEMBER   SAMUEL K. ROTHSTEIN   HARRY WEISBORD
FRANZ WINKLER

NORTH AMERICAN JEWISH COUNCIL   CRAIG WASSERMAN

UNION OF AMERICAN HEBREW CONGREGATIONS   RABBI LEONARD A. SCHOOLMAN

UNITED SYNAGOGUE OF AMERICA   MR. JEAN LEWIS   SIMON SCHWARTZ
DAVID ZUCKER